D1101973

# Russia 'n' Roll!

The Legends of Rock 'n' Roll –
from a Russian perspective

by

Richard Hume

**DORRANCE**
PUBLISHING CO
EST. 1920
PITTSBURGH, PENNSYLVANIA 15238

The contents of this work, including, but not limited to, the accuracy of events, people, and places depicted; opinions expressed; permission to use previously published materials included; and any advice given or actions advocated are solely the responsibility of the author, who assumes all liability for said work and indemnifies the publisher against any claims stemming from publication of the work.

All Rights Reserved
Copyright © 2016 by Richard Hume

No part of this book may be reproduced or transmitted, downloaded, distributed, reverse engineered, or stored in or introduced into any information storage and retrieval system, in any form or by any means, including photocopying and recording, whether electronic or mechanical, now known or hereinafter invented without permission in writing from the publisher.

Dorrance Publishing Co
585 Alpha Drive
Pittsburgh, PA 15238
Visit our website at *www.dorrancebookstore.com*

ISBN: 978-1-4809-3094-0
eISBN: 978-1-4809-3117-6

THIS ARTICLE
AND ALL THE OTHERS IN THIS BOOK,
FIRST APPEARED IN
"MAGGIE'S BLUE SUEDE NEWS,"
THE UK ROCK 'N' ROLL MAGAZINE.

*Thanks to Sergey, Misha, Vicki and Valeria for some of the photos.*
*Thanks to Grant and Tamara, for their contribution to rock'n'roll in Moscow.*
*And to my Russian rockin' friends, for their support and encouragement*
*for my writings about rock 'n' roll and also for their being part*
*of our Great Rock 'n' Roll Culture, Keep Rockin'!*

# Contents

September 2012 - ROCKIN' IN RUSSIA! . . . . . . . . . . . . . . . . . . . . . . . . . . . 1

October 2012 - REAL HOT ROCKIN' IN RUSSIA . . . . . . . . . . . . . . . . . . . . . 5

November 2012 - HITTING THE REEFS! . . . . . . . . . . . . . . . . . . . . . . . . . . 9

December 2012 - ROCKABILLY RULES OK – IN MOSCOW! . . . . . . . . . . . . 13

January 2013 - HITTING THE HIGH NOTES . . . . . . . . . . . . . . . . . . . . . . 17

February 2013 - SWEET AND HOT ! . . . . . . . . . . . . . . . . . . . . . . . . . . . 19

March 2013 - JIVE, JIVE, JIVE ! . . . . . . . . . . . . . . . . . . . . . . . . . . . . . 23

April 2013 - FRUITY AND DELICIOUS ! . . . . . . . . . . . . . . . . . . . . . . . . 27

May 2013 - GET YOUR KICKS ON ROUTE...67! . . . . . . . . . . . . . . . . . . 31

June 2013 - RAW AND UNCUT . . . . . . . . . . . . . . . . . . . . . . . . . . . . . 35

July 2013 1957 - THE BIRTH OF RUSSIAN ROCK'N'ROLL . . . . . . . . . . . 39

August 2013 - HAIL TO THE KING – IN RUSSIA ! . . . . . . . . . . . . . . . . . 43

September 2013-THE RUSSIAN "KILLER" ! . . . . . . . . . . . . . . . . . . . . . . 47

October 2013 - THE KILLER, THE ONE AND ONLY . . . . . . . . . . . . . . . 49

November 2013 - CHUCK BERRY – STILL MOTORVATIN'! . . . . . . . . . . 51

December 2013 - THE GREATEST (ROCK'N'ROLL) SHOW! . . . . . . . . . . . 55

January 2014 - THE RETURN OF THE REEFS! . . . . . . . . . . . . . . . . . . . 59

February 2014 - THE ONE AND ONLY . . . . . . . . . . . . . . . . . . . . . . . . . 63

March 2014 - THE GREATEST MARCH . . . . . . . . . . . . . . . . . . . . . . . 67

April 2014 - WALK ON THE WILD SIDE . . . . . . . . . . . . . . . . . . . . . . 71

May 2014 - THE QUASAR OF ROCK'N'ROLL! . . . . . . . . . . . . . . . . . . 75

June 2014 - THE WILDEST CAT . . . . . . . . . . . . . . . . . . . . . . . . . . . . 79

July 2014 - A ROCK'N'ROLL HOME – IN RUSSIA! . . . . . . . . . . . . . . . 85

August 2014 - THE FIRST ROCK'N'ROLL SUPERSTAR . . . . . . . . . . . . . 89

September 2014-THE MONSTER RAVING LOONY OF ROCK 'n' ROLL . . . . . 93

October 2014 - THE MONSTER RAVING LOONY – TAKE 2! . . . . . . . . . . 97

November 2014- THE COMEDY KING OF ROCK'N'ROLL . . . . . . . . . . . . 103

December 2014 - DANCE TO THE GUITAR MAN . . . . . . . . . . . . . . . . . 109

January 2015 - THE UK ROCKABILLY RAVE – RUSSIAN STYLE! . . . . . . 115

February 2015 - THE MOVIE THAT ROCKED BRITAIN . . . . . . . . . . . . . 119

March 2015 - SWEET AND HOT – TAKE TWO! . . . . . . . . . . . . . . . . . 125

April 2015 - A ROCK'N'ROLL LIFE  . . . . . . . . . . . . . . . . . . . . . . . . . . . . . . . 131

May 2015 - SOMETHIN' ELSE  . . . . . . . . . . . . . . . . . . . . . . . . . . . . . . . . . . . 137

June 2015 - THE HOTTEST ROCKIN' CHICK OF THEM ALL!  . . . . . . . . 143

July 2015  - THE TRUE KING OF ROCKABILLY . . . . . . . . . . . . . . . . . . . . 149

August 2015  - THE LIFE AND TIMES OF A RUSSIAN LEGEND. . . . . . . 155

September 2015- THE ORIGINAL REBEL  . . . . . . . . . . . . . . . . . . . . . . . . . 163

October 2015 - RUSSIA'S WILDEST CAT . . . . . . . . . . . . . . . . . . . . . . . . . . 169

November 2015 - RED AND ROCKIN'. . . . . . . . . . . . . . . . . . . . . . . . . . . . . 177

September 2012

# ROCKIN' IN RUSSIA!

Rock'n'roll is alive and kickin' in Russia! Russia and especially Moscow is one of the fastest growing rock 'n' roll scenes in the world.

The clientele are predominantly young people. Russia has much fewer older rockers going back to the 50s or our UK Revival period of the 70s: The Communist Party and the history of the Soviet Union didn't encourage such capitalist culture. I left the UK to live and work in Russia in August 2004. The contrast that immediately struck me most between the rock'n'roll in the 2 countries was the different generations who follow the great music. Here in Russia young people are joining and staying with it. How Russian rock'n'roll got to this healthy position is linked to Russia's recent history.

## THE HISTORY

During the 1950s in the USSR some people were playing rock'n'roll records but mainly at home. Then in 1957 the Soviet authorities organised a huge youth and student festival in Moscow. They invited musicians from the USA and the UK to come and play, comprising mainly rock'n'roll and jazz bands. One notable performer was none other than Tommy Steele! The influence of this festival on some young Russians was immense. It kick-started a significant youth culture movement in Russia, centred on St Petersburg and Moscow.

But the communist authorities made it clear that whilst they were happy to allow a one-off festival, fraternising with the "class enemy" and engaging in "decadent" capitalist culture was still forbidden. However after this festival some of the youth refused to be intimidated and began a youth culture of their own. Foremost in this Movement from the early 60s was the Stilyagi (based on the Russian word for "style"). They were more or less the first real rock-'n'rollers in Russia. Their style was not 100% rock'n'roll - they also listened to and followed other brands of music such as jazz – and this was also reflected in their style of clothing. But it was close enough to establish them as the original Russian youth rebels.

This rebellion continued up to and into the period of Glasnost and Perestroika which began in the mid-80s (These were the terms used for the momentous changes in the Soviet Union under Mikhail Gorbachev).

And from 1979 a new phenomenon – a group openly calling themselves Teddy Boys! Based in St Petersburg they were formed from out of the Stilyagi movement. In 1982 they formed their own club "the Leningrad Teddy Boys Club", based in the centre of the city. Their unofficial "leader" was Anton "Teddy". He was an icon amongst the youth at that time and a well known figure in cultural circles during the 80s. The Teddy Boys' Club was very knowledgeable on western youth culture and were instrumental in giving information and advice to the rockabilly rebels of that period, on such things as the correct style of dress, authentic sound of music, etc.

The Teddy Boy Club lasted up to 1984. Unlike in the UK, the youth identities were much more fluid: By the mid-80s these Teds who were still very much part of the Stilyagi culture had adopted other styles such as punk, biker, rockabilly or new wave, etc.

In the 90s in true youth culture tradition the Stilyagi and the Rockabillies had serious feuds and fights against each other! This included many criminal

arrests, mainly in St Petersburg. Russian friends who lived through those times tell me this violence was inspired mainly by what the 2 groups had learned about British rock history e.g. 50s Teddy Boys' aggression, Mods vs. Rockers, Teds / Rockabillies vs. Punks

/ Skinheads, etc. In other words they felt this was what they were expected to do. So this was another famous British export!

These Russian pioneers of youth culture deserve praise. Supporting rock-'n'roll (and even more so in the period before Glasnost and Perestroika) at that time carried dangers with the authorities so they were real rock'n'roll revolutionaries. Their rebellion was social, not political.

The history of the old Soviet Union meant that most members of the bands never grew up with the authentic r'n'r sound like we did in the UK i.e. listening to it on the radio, TV, or other mass media outlets. So what they did was play and re-play vinyls of the original r'n'r recordings when they became more available from the 1980s onwards. After countless hours of such "homework" the musicians finally acquired the authentic sound, adding on their own individual styles. And the results were impressive.

### ROCK'N'ROLL IN RUSSIA NOW

The best bands here in Russia are not just cheap imitations of the Western sound - they have their own style and stand up in comparison with all but the elite bands in the West. The quality of the best groups here is excellent. See what I mean by checking out the following great Russian Bands on www.youtube.com (in the youtube search engine box add "Moscow" after each band's name):

**STRESSOR - GREAT PRETENDERS - BEAT DEVILS - ALLIGA-
TORS - CORAL REEFS – RAW CATS 88 – LEX AND TEAM**

So hail Russian rock'n'roll, an important member of the World's rock'n'roll
family!

Finally, a totally unrelated rock'n'roll joke, dedicated to a band that allegedly
did rock'n'roll no favours –

*Q: What were the worst words ever said in rock and roll?*
*A: "How about we let Ringo sing one."*

# REAL HOT ROCKIN' IN RUSSIA

Esse Jazz Café, Moscow; 21st July

In my article on Russian rock'n'roll in the last issue of the magazine, I reported on the very high quality of the bands here. Here's an excellent example:

Vladimir Pankratov and Real Hot BBQ are a 4 piece, playing hot, smokin' r'n'r. Their style is authentic 50s', not just their sound but their look too. They're relatively new, the band formed in 2010, but they've become rock'n'roll icons in Moscow and Russia.

Vladimir is the leader and vocalist, plus plays rhythm guitar and piano. He has real charisma on stage. It's clear from his stage performance that he's spent a lot of time studying the 50s style and the results are impressive. He is an actor and has also directed films. His father Alexander Pankratov is a very famous Russian actor and film director.

The band have regular gigs at many of the high prestige clubs in Moscow. One of the most notable of these is the Esse Jazz Café in the centre of Moscow, a premier venue for jazz and rock'n'roll events. I run many of my rock'n'roll jive dance classes there and on 21st July my class at the Café preceded the band coming on stage. One benefit of these classes is teaching non-dancers the basics, giving them the opportunity to try out what they've learned later on in the evening (instead of sitting and watching and wishing they could get out on the dance floor and jive!). And to be sure, the dance floor was fully occupied all evening.

On the night, my favourite tracks from the band were "Nervous Breakdown", "Do what you did", "Too much loving" and "Life begins at 4 O'Clock", all served up in the authentic 50s style. Plus they can slow it down too while maintaining that rock'n'roll feel, witness "It's only make believe" and "The

treasure of love". And maybe my number one favourite from their set is "Straight skirt", a track the group have really sort of made their own – I love it!

Thankfully the band are not content to stick to the same song list and are continually adding to it with new material. One of the first questions I ever asked the group was, why not "Red Hot BBQ"? They advised it was because another group somewhere in the world has already taken that name, and the guys wanna be original and unique!

The audience, which mainly comprised followers of the band, dancers, plus regular customers of the Café some of whom hadn't seen the group before, enjoyed the whole event hugely. If Russian people like something they're very open with their feelings. So to coin a phrase, "the joint was jumpin'".

In addition to Vladimir, their line-up comprises Oleg Ivanin on lead guitar, Michael Averyanov on double bass and Andrey Laptev on drums. Oleg has a distinguished history in Russian rock'n'roll, chiefly as lead guitarist for many years now for the Moscow rockabilly band the Great Pretenders. Andrey is a more recent musician on the scene, he's rockabilly to his bones as well as being a bit of a dancer. Plus their friends of mine; so I hope Andrey won't mind if I throw in a couple of drummer jokes:

*"What do you call someone who hangs out with musicians?
A drummer."*

*"Did you hear about the time the bass player locked his keys in the car? It took two hours to get the drummer out."*

As we're over a thousand miles away from the UK, here's one way you can check out the group. Go to youtube and in the search box type "Vladimir Pankratov and Real Hot BBQ" and see what you think. For example, type in "Richard Hume and Real Hot BBQ" and you'll see a video of a concert they did in June this year at the same venue.

So a great evening's entertainment was had by all on 21/07/12. Real hot r'n'r, grilled on a roasting rock'n'roll barbeque. Smokin'!

Richard Hume
Moscow

### Grand Bourbon Street, Moscow; 18th August

# HITTING THE REEFS!

Who is the best jive and swing band in the World ? That could be the focus of a very interesting debate; as far as the UK is concerned my vote would go to the Jive Aces. But here's a much, much easier question – who are the best jive and swing band in Russian and Eastern Europe ? The simple answer is – the Coral Reefs. Or in Russian, that translates into "Coralaviye Reefiy.

The location for their concert on 18th August, "Grand Bourbon Street", is one of the best music and rock'n'roll venues in Moscow. And as you can guess from the name one of their specialities is a huge choice of whiskies at the bar, at low prices!

The Reefs are an 8 piece outfit. The line-up features keyboards, lead guitar, bass guitar, trumpet, trombone, saxophone and drums. Their leader is the singer Kirill Sukhomlikov. Kirill has huge presence on stage; not only his voice, but he generates a lot of charisma. He studied acting at University and this is reflected in his stage performance; he puts on a real show. Plus it's always a pleasure to jive dance with his wife at their concerts! She's a dance graduate from University and her dancing reflects it.

Like the Jive Aces they are not 100% pure rock'n'roll, but have very strong rock'n'roll influences in their music. The band composes many of it's own songs. The main composer of their tunes is the keyboard player

Mikhail Deryabin. The inspiration for coming up with most of the lyrics is Kirill. Mikhail assures everyone he hears the new tunes in his sleep and then writes down the music for them when he wakes up! In any event the end result really works – their musical compositions are of exceptional quality. Their set mixes their own material with their interpretation of existing musical standards.

They perform both in English and Russian, depending on what it is their singing. Their own compositions are also either in Russian or English. My favourites from their own songs at the gig on the night were "Simply Winter", "Midnight fate", "That day" and "Eyes of night lamps", a mixture of fast and slow numbers. Of the existing standards, I think I was most impressed with their versions of "Speedy Gonzales", "Whole Lotta Shakin' " and "Americano": all done in the Reefs' inimitable rockin' style. Smokin'!

And here's a special attraction the Reefs possess: Their bassist Eleanora Hayrapetyan, a relatively recent acquisition to the band, not only plays exceptionally well but she's absolutely stunning to look at! Makes me wish I was 30 years younger :)) And that's saying something in Russia: From my own experience working in other countries like the USA, Russian women are definitely the most beautiful in the world. Sorry all you British ladies but it's true!

The band are friends of mine and it's always a pleasure to co-operate with them at their gigs. I usually start their concerts with a dance master class and the band comes on stage immediately following the class. As they are friends, I hope they won't mind me including the following musician jokes ……..

*What's the first thing a musician says at work?*
*"Would you like fries with that?"*

*Why do musicians have to be awake by six o'clock?*
*Because most shops close by six thirty.*

Have a look and listen to the Reefs yourselves and see what you think! Go to-
http://www.rify.ru/video.html

Thank you to the Coral Reefs for a great night at Grand Bourbon Street; hot jive, swing and rock'n'roll from the best band of the genre in Russia!

# ROCKABILLY RULES OK – IN MOSCOW!
## Tramplin Club, Moscow, 20th October

Rockabilly music, since its birth in the 1950s in the Southern States of the USA, has found its way to many places around the world. Nowhere more so than here in the land of the Old Curtain and in particular in Moscow.

One of the greatest exponents of this brand of rock'n'roll in Russia played the Tramplin Club in Moscow on 20th October. The Great Pretenders are a 4-piece outfit with a long pedigree. Formed in 1995, they're icons on the rockabilly scene here. Their basic style i.e. pure, authentic rockabilly, hasn't changed, but as a group they have developed and progressed over the years.

Only one original remains from the starting up of 1995: Sergey Kuteynikov founded the group and is still the lead vocalist and rhythm guitarist. He got the rockabilly bug back in the 1980s when as a small boy his family lived in San Francisco for 3 years – his Dad was a diplomat for the Soviet mission there. It enabled Sergey to listen to rockabilly much more freely than he would have been able to in the old USSR. This experience stayed with him all his life. As a teenager he set up a rockabilly club in Moscow, calling it the Sharks Club and out of this sprang the beginnings of the Great Pretenders.

Sergey is a friend of mine and told me a story from the early days of the Pretenders:

One of their earliest gigs back then was at a jazz club called the Blue Bird. The club had a reputation as a relaxed laid back jazz venue. So the promoter advertised the gig as the opportunity for a "relaxed, laid back evening", not quite realising rockabilly Pretenders-style is not your average easy on the ear jazz. Not only the raucous music that night gave some of the club patrons rather a shock …

A group of young skinheads turned up unexpectedly at the club and a huge fight ensued between them and the rockabilly crew from the Sharks Club (the pretext for the fight was over the favours of a young woman). The gig ended in mayhem, including the promoter running off without paying the band. In Russian rockabilly folklore, they still remember that "relaxed, laid back evening" back in the 1990s! Russian rockabilly had arrived with a bang.

At the Tramplin club on 20th October 2012, a large audience of rock'n'rollers were not disappointed. The band's set included some of their favourites. Teddy Boy Boogie is one of mine: The Pretenders' version is the nearest you'll ever get to Crazy Cavan's, this side of the Severn Bridge! "Let's beat the Mods" is the group's own composition and yes it harks back to the old 60's warfare between mods and rockers. It's a great number, predictably being a big favourite amongst the bikers over here "descended" from the old rockers. Two other numbers they have especially made their own and which they played on the night, were "Cruisin'" and "Dance to the bop". Re. the latter, anything with a Gene Vincent connection is alright by me!

Those readers with a good memory will remember that my article in the magazine 2 months ago featured the group Real Hot BBQ. As I mentioned in that article, Oleg Ivanin is the lead guitarist for that band too as well as the Pretenders. He's a guitarist in demand! He plays great rockabilly and is free of the egotism that accompanies some lead guitarists …

*"How many guitar players does it take to change a light bulb?*
*Twelve. One to change the bulb and eleven to say they could do it better."*

So it was another Great night of rockabilly on 20th from the band with no airs or Pretences. Here's to the Great Pretenders – great rockabilly, from a country that knows how to Rock!

# HITTING THE HIGH NOTES

### Esse Jazz Café, Moscow – Saturday 17th November

My article this month confirms the strength of Russian rockabilly. Here's a band that knows how to hit the high notes (or tones) …

The HiTones are a relatively new four-piece outfit, comprising a lead guitar, acoustic guitar, upright bass and drums. They hail from Moscow. They've become hugely popular on the rock'n'roll scene in Russia, particularly amongst the followers of rockabilly. Their leader is vocalist and acoustic guitar Alexey Schukin. He founded the group in 2010 with the aim to play authentic 50's music. Alexey says their musical inspiration comes from the likes of Johnny Burnett, the Delta Bombers, Eddy and the Backfires and the Rhythm Shakers.

On 17th November the band played the Esse Café, one of the premier rock'n'roll venues in Moscow. A full crowd comprised rock'n'rollers, dancers and regular café patrons – none were disappointed! It was a great evening of hard drivin' 50's rockabilly.

A key element of the group is lead guitar Vladimir Khoruzhiy, one of the best guitarists in Russia. He also does the odd harmonica number. The bassist Alexey Nikitin and the drummer Vladimir Malashonok provide the solid rockabilly beat that helps give them that authentic sound. Malashonok is a veteran of many Russian bands: He's a fine musician, despite what they say about drummers …

*What's the difference between a drummer and a Podiatrist?*
*A. The Podiatrist bucks up your feet, whereas the drummer...*

*What's the similarity between a drummer and a philosopher?*
*A: They both perceive time as an abstract concept.*

But Schukin is the real leader, not least with his presence on stage. He puts on a real performance. It's clear he's done a lot of studying to get that raw, authentic rockabilly feel.

The band started off covering versions of popular hits, but in 2011 The Hitones started composing their own original songs. This was followed in March 2012 with the release of a single, "I'm gonna leave you". The release of a full length CD is planned for early next year.

On the night, my favourite cover versions that the band played included "Everybody's movin", "Long blonde hair" and "Let's go boppin' tonight". Of their own compositions, I liked especially "I'm gonna leave you", "Baby please come back" and "Electric dreamer". Their set is more or less a 50 / 50 balance between original and cover versions.

Have a listen to the band yourself and see what you think. Go to youtube and type "HiTones Moscow' in the search engine box. Or go to their home page at http://www.reverbnation.com/hitonesrussia

And sit back and listen to hard drivin' rockabilly, Moscow-style!

# SWEET AND HOT!

This month let me introduce to you from Moscow, something sweet and delicious ...

The Marshmallows are a hugely exciting group on the Russian rock'n'roll scene. The musicians comprise a guitar, bassist and drummer, but it is the other 3 members of the 6-piece who are the real stars:

They are 3 beautiful young Russian female singers, who perform excellent 50's style rock'n'roll. They're brilliant. They're a real phenomenon on the rockin' scene here.

This month I'm gonna present the bulk of my article in a different way ...

Nadya Kunareva, who is one of these 3 fabulous singers, wrote a piece for me for this article, describing the style and the history of the band. I could never have written it so well. All I had to do was translate it for you from her Russian text! So here is Nadya's presentation of the band, written in a way only a beautiful, intelligent young Russian woman can ...

**"Marshmallows – the immodest charm of a rock'n'roll:**

Allow me to present, on the Moscow scene, a rock'n'roll collective in the authentic 50s style.

Fronting the band are a trio of bright vocalists, delightful to the naked eye - Masha Nosova, Julia Chuguev and myself Nadya Kunareva. We are backed by the strong shoulders of 3 young men, our musicians: Dmitriy Smagin (guitar), Andrey Laptev (drums) and Vladimir Manturov (contrabass).

If you aren't indifferent to model pin-up posters and your heart warms to the sound of a needle rustling on an old vinyl playing rockabilly, swing, rock'n'roll, country, boogie and a heap of other incendiary rhythms … If such icons as Imelda May, Brenda Lee, Wanda Jackson or Janis Martin are not just names to you … And if you not against spending an evening in the company of charming young women who prefer scarlet lipstick and high heels as their style of fashion – then Welcome to Party Marshmallows!

The Marshmallows began in 2011 and made an immediate impact on the Russian scene. For those "who like it hot", this band is for you – we express music, power, mood and pleasure. We play the biggest rock'n'roll venues in Russia, particularly at our home base in

Moscow. We are regular performers at such venues as Radio City, Bilingua, Café Blues, Chicago, Glastonberry, the Double Bourbon and the Esse Jazz Café.

Why the name "Marshmallows" ? Because we are like small air pillows with a rich taste. And above all because we believe all marshmallows should be heated up and served hot. We like it hot!"

Thank you, Nadya. All three of the vocalists are thankfully free of the egotism that accompanies some female singers –

*"How many female vocalists does it take to change a light bulb ?*
*One. She holds the bulb and the world revolves around her."*

Have a look at the Marshmallows yourself and see what you think. Go to their facebook page at http://www.facebook.com/MarshmallowsMoscow? ref=ts&fref=ts or check them out on youtube – type "Marshmallows rock-'n'roll" in the search box.

**The Marshmallows, hot music with a soft centre!**

# JIVE, JIVE, JIVE!

This month I'm gonna take time out from telling you about the excellent rock'n'roll bands here in Russia, to focus on the dancing side of things. In particular, wanna tell you about something unique in rock'n'roll dancing. And it's happening right here in Russia.

For any group to describe itself as unique is a dangerous claim to make – there's usually someone who comes forward to say they're doing the same thing. But Moscow-based Co-op Jive can justly claim to be the only free co-operative that exists to "link, help and support rock'n'roll jive dancers."

I set up the co-operative in the 1980s when I lived and worked in the UK, as an antidote to the commercialism of dance schools. I don't blame dance schools for being commercial – people have to make a living. But it seemed to me that dancers were being pushed in a direction where they didn't want to go.

Dance schools seemed to be coming up with new steps, in order to run more and more classes, to make more money from people without really considering what most dancers really wanted – the opportunity to learn the basic skills needed to dance socially.

Setting up the co-operative enabled me to combine something I really believe in with something I really enjoy. Co-operatives exist to make a positive contribution to people's lives and we want to give people the freedom to really dance with feeling and enjoy the music. In other words, there is less emphasis on more and more dance steps. We want to give dancers the skills to be able to get out on the dance floor and enjoy themselves, rather than getting them to pay for more and more classes to learn more and more steps.

The co-operative has been based in Moscow since 2004 when I moved to Russia to live and work. Prior to that I ran the co-operative for many years in the UK. We organise rock'n'roll dance and music events on a weekly basis (I've got a full-time job, so once a week is the maximum I can do), including free dance classes: They are bi-lingual i.e. taught in English and Russian. All the events we are involved in are non-profit making. Also anyone anywhere in the world can contact the co-operative, for details about where to dance in their area of the world. More details about all this are available on my website at www.coopjive.co.uk

The first dance class I ever attended was many years ago. I still remember it. I went along to a dance class at Covent Garden in London. It turned out to be a jitterbug class which was not exactly what I was looking for. I'd had a tough day at work, arrived late, felt really out of place and was about to get up and leave.

A young woman then came across and encouraged me to have a go (she had obviously noticed the unhappy look on my face!). I haven't stopped dancing since. I only saw that young woman once more, at the next class and didn't get a chance to talk to her. I never saw her again, but I still quietly thank her for getting me started. You can't always return a favour but you can pass it on and that's what I hope the dance co-operative has been able to do.

# FRUITY AND DELICIOUS!

This month I'd like to introduce you to another excellent Russian band, whose style and sound is very much a cocktail.

Avocado are a 4-piece band, comprising a vocalist, violinist, guitar and contrabass / bass guitar. This itself suggests a group which, although strong in rock'n'roll influences, has a more mixed sound to it. The best way to describe them is a mix of swing and rock'n'roll.

The biggest star of Avocado is unquestionably the singer Alexandra Esakova. She looks real good on stage, but above all her voice is beautiful and special and she has real charisma.

Another feature of the group which makes it unusual is the prominence of the violinist Elizabeth

Smirnova. Guitarist Pavel Vlasov and bass guitar Andrey Artiomov complete the regular line-up. In addition, Yaroslav Andreev is their usual drummer for their gigs.

Andrey is the acknowledged leader of the group and handles most of the bookings, publicity, and business side of things. From my experience I can confirm he's very efficient in this area; nothing is forgotten in his preparation for gigs!

The band's history goes back to 2006, when they started performing at  some of the premier concert venues in Moscow. Artiomov founded the group and he's the only remaining survivor from the original line-up. The sound and style of Avocado has undergone significant changes over time. I remember seeing them in their early days; their singer then was another real good lookin' star with a wonderful voice and personality on stage, Maria Homenko. Her departure, along with other personnel, changed the band's style to one with more swing and less rock'n'roll. But the rock'n'roll is still there and the sound, although different, is still something special.

The group's play list comprises a mixture of their own compositions and musical standards. Again, it is Artiomov who does the composing, creating the tunes as well as the lyrics. As the titles of their own compositions would mean little to UK ears, here's some of the standards they like to play live: That's alright Mama, Stupid Cupid, Fever, Route 66, Kansas City and My Boy Elvis. Of these, I guess my favourite when seeing them perform is "My Boy Elvis" – smokin'!

Check the band out on youtube – type in "Avocado Band Russia" in the search engine and have a look and listen.

So here's to Avocado, a nice of bunch of individuals with a great sound and an impressive stage performance; one more example of the hot, rockin' quality of Russian music!

And to round off this article, just to say I'm pleased that the articles in the magazine covering what's happening on the rock'n'roll scene outside the UK, prompted some readers to write to the editor about them. Of course some were not exactly positive on the subject, but it was good that some readers felt strongly enough about it to write. Long live Rock'n'Roll throughout the planet – let's take over the World!

# GET YOUR KICKS ON ROUTE ..... 67!

This month let me take you to the wilder side of Russian rock'n'roll. This story is based not in the capital Moscow, where I live and work, but in Smolensk, a city near the country's western border.

The band is Route 67. For those of you who know your American musical history, nope they haven't got the number wrong. Russia is divided numerically into different regions and Smolensk is in region 67, just one digit away from that famous highway. But of course Route 66 is the inspiration for their name.

Their style is what we'd call neo-rockabilly, somewhere between rockabilly and psychobilly. That may not be everyone's cup of tea, but there's no doubt this band is real good at what they do. Hard drivin' rock'n'roll which takes no prisoners; that kind of sums up the style and attitude of the group. In the October issue of the magazine, I reviewed their first CD which had just been issued, "Sinful Way" on Crazy Love records. It's a smokin' CD, hard drivin' neo-rockabilly from the start to the finish, comprising their own compositions - on the CD only one track is a cover version.

As the names of their own songs would mean little to western audiences, here's a flavor of the kind of cover versions they perform on stage:

Twenty flight rock, Rockabilly boogie, Oh boy, Blue jean bop, Matchbox, Summertime blues, I'm ready; all performed in the neo-rockabilly style.

The band have been going since 2007 and the 2 main elements have not changed since then; Vladimir Katulsky, lead guitar / vocal and Andrey Sheshero, upright bass and support vocalist, the core of the band, are still there. Only the drummers have changed – they're now with their third drummer, Andrey Moiseenkov. Vladimir composes the group's songs, with a bit of help from Andrey.

Vladimir is a good friend of mine and told me something that took place at one of their concerts in west Russia. The gig was at Voronezh, not too far from Smolensk and I wasn't at the event myself, but here's what happened:

During their concerts the group do different kinds of visual effects on stage. For example, often Vladimir plays the guitar while standing on the upright bass. At this concert in Voronezh, as usual during one of the songs (it was Jack the Ripper) he played the guitar while standing on the bass, then slipped and suddenly ........ fell right into the face of the instrument! The bass was completely smashed and destroyed. It was awful for Vlad and of course the bass player. Vlad fell to the floor, but kept the guitar in his hands. Fortunately it was the last song of the concert and they finished the number with just the drummer playing.

But …. the crowd was ecstatic! They really went wild with the excitement of what had happened!

Rock'n'roll fans from other cities in Russia learned very quickly about what had occurred. Soon after, at another concert, as the band did their sound check at the beginning, a guy came up to the stage and asked them, "we heard about your fantastic show in Voronezh. Please can you destroy your upright bass today for us ?" This guy seriously thought, as did others, that this destruction was part of the act! Maybe they'd been watching too many videos of "the Who". The band now call this event "the story of the upright bass destroyers"!

Thanks to the wonders of the internet, you can have a look at the group yourself and see what you think. Go to youtube and type "Route 67 Russia" in the search engine.

So here's to Route 67. Moscow is the cultural capital of Russian rock'n'roll, but this band from Smolensk are livin' proof that although the capital for sure is the leader, there are other competitors in the race!

# RAW AND UNCUT

This month, am gonna introduce you to an iconic group in Russian rock'n'roll.

Raw Cats 88 are a four piece outfit based in Moscow, formed in 2004. At the present time they are amongst the most famous groups in Russia, with a huge following.

There are 2 original members of the band going back to 2004; Keyboards and lead vocal Valery Setkin and drummer Stas Mikosho. Dimitriy Smagin on guitar / vocal and Denis Ovchinnikov on double bass complete the line-up.

Any discussion of the band needs to start with Setkin. He is to say the least a larger than life figure and the real star. The best way to describe his style as a performer is, a mixture of Elvis and Jerry Lee. He not only has a great voice and keyboard excellence, but also displays charisma and character on stage.

At times he's slamming down on the keyboards in the manner of Jerry Lee. Then he's singing in the style of Elvis. It's not a copy act, but an authentic rock'n'roll style that is heavily influenced by those 2 icons.

There are quite a few stories about him, linked to the history of the band. Most of the best ones relate to alcohol, women and strippers! Many of these I could not relate to you in a family magazine like this one! But here is one I can …

One of the band's biggest fans is a gorgeous looking young Russian woman, who goes to see them perform not only in Moscow but other cities in Russia. On one occasion the group were performing in Tver (a city about 200 miles from the capital) and once again the young lady was there to see them. But the excitement of the occasion must have got to her and half way through the band's set she proceeded to do a full blown strip tease act, while the group were playing "you can leave your hat on" (which is all she did keep on). Apparently it was an unforgettable performance! The group kept on playing during this strip (I admire their professionalism), but 2 of the club's security guards after the song collected all her clothes and threw her and her attire out of the club. By the way the saddest part of this story is that I was not at the concert to see this exotic cabaret!

But the tale has a happy ending. During the intermission Setkin, who was feeling very sorry for the young fan, discovered that their changing room backed onto the street. So he was able to smuggle the girl back into the club. She was eternally grateful and (although I have not been lucky enough to be at the right concerts to see one yet!) occasionally she repeats her raunchy stage act at Raw Cats' gigs.

As their own compositions would mean little to Western ears, here are some of the standards they often cover on stage;

Viva Las Vegas, Runaway, Sweet Home Alabama, Burning Love, Ring of fire, A little less conversation, You got it, Great balls of fire and Rock this town. Their version of Viva Las Vegas is particularly impressive on stage – best one I've heard, except for the King's of course.

What is personally rewarding (I'm sure other veteran rockers can relate to this) is to witness over the years how a band develops and advances. I moved to Moscow the same year the Raw Cats were formed. Over the last 9 years, going to their gigs, I've seen their progression from a good group into a great one.

Why the name "Raw Cats 88"? Valeri advised me it derives from the classic song "Rocket 88", which was one of the first rock'n'roll numbers he ever heard and helped to get him hooked on the great music as a young boy.

You can check out the band yourself. Go to youtube and type "Raw Cats 88" in the search engine box. Hail the Raw Cats - as their name implies, the music is raw with a hard edge!

# 1957 – THE BIRTH

# OF RUSSIAN ROCK'N'ROLL

This month let me take you on a journey into rock'n'roll history. The year is 1957. Something happened that year which changed rock'n'roll forever … in Russia!

First the background:

During the 1950s in the USSR some people were playing early rock'n'roll records but nearly always at home. Fearful of what the communist authorities would do when confronted with this "decadent" western culture (remember this was the height of the Cold War), no-one dared to do any more than that.

But then it happened. In 1957 the Soviet authorities organised a huge youth and student festival in Moscow. They invited musicians from the USA, comprising mainly rock'n'roll and jazz bands, to come and play at the festival.

Of course this was a propaganda event by the Soviets. It was seen by them as a way to present themselves as open-minded and open to the world, at the

same time ensuring they closely controlled the event and got maximum propaganda value out of it. And also the bands quoted above who were invited to the event were only a small part of it. Most of the active participants were card carrying young Russian communists happy to help further the "socialist" cause, who at the festival engaged in marching in parades or watching and listening to traditional folk music. And most of the young foreigners invited to the festival (around 34,000 came in total) were generally communist party members or communist sympathisers. The United States government at the time declared the Festival was part of a publicity campaign, to try and offset the losses in the "propaganda war" incurred by the Soviet Union during its suppression of the Hungarian uprising the previous year.

But ... the script didn't go according to plan. Many young Russians, men and women, became enthused as they watched the bands performing. And guess who came over from the UK to perform; none other than Tommy Steele! It would be very interesting to know what Tommy's impressions were of it all and if he got the chance to inter-act with some of the young Russians attending the concert.

Some Russians paid a price: Some of the young Muscovite women tried to get to know more about this exciting culture by chatting to the American musicians during the festival and the American men and the Russian women exchanged their experiences in their respective countries. Later the authorities singled out these women and the Militsia (Russian police) arrested them. Their hair was cut and their dresses torn. In other words they were publicly humiliated. It was a clear signal from the government that while they were happy to allow a one-off festival, fraternising with the "class enemy" was still forbidden.

The influence of this festival on some young Russians was immense. It kick-started a significant movement in Russia, centred on Leningrad (since re-named St Petersburg) and Moscow. Most of these rebels centred themselves around a movement they called "Stilyagi", derived from the Russian word for "style". After the festival they refused to be intimidated and began a youth culture of their own.

Foremost in this history as it developed from the 1950s onwards, was again the Stilyagi. They were more or less the first real rock'n'rollers in Russia. Their style was not 100% rock'n'roll - they also listened to and followed other brands of music such as jazz – and this was also reflected in their style of clothing. But it was close enough to establish them as the original Russian youth rebels. Their rebellion was social, not political.

These young Russians deserve praise. They were risking persecution by the authorities for continuing to follow this culture, after they had seen something at the festival in 1957 that they didn't want to lose. I came to live and work in Russia in 2004 and I can remember being shown propaganda films made in the 1950s and 1960s by the Russian authorities, depicting these young rebels as hooligans and layabouts. These same clips also showed well dressed and well behaved young Russian communist men and women, as wonderful examples of what young people should be like! I enjoyed watching the films hugely – really funny!

With the momentous changes in Russia in the 1980s, things started to "loosen up" for the Stilyagi and the collapse of the Soviet Union by the beginning of the 1990s made things much easier for them to follow their chosen life style.

So it was that a festival organised by the communist government in the Soviet Union at the height of the Cold War, inadvertently kick-started a rock-'n'roll revolution.

Today in Moscow you can visit a famous café / restaurant, located right next to Red Square. It's called "Stalovaya 57" (Stalovaya in Russian means eating place) and is dedicated to that 1957 festival. All the décor, right down to a 1950s juke box, is an authentic re-creation of 1957. Stalovaya 57 is a well known landmark in Moscow and is further evidence of the importance of that

1957 Festival on the history of Russian youth culture. When I brought the UK rock'n'roll group Furious to Moscow to perform on 2 occasions, I made a point of taking them to the restaurant, to give them a taste of Russian rock-'n'roll history.

So here's to those early Russian rock'n'roll pioneers back in the 1950s, who certainly had it tougher than their counterparts in the West, in their efforts to grow and preserve their rock'n'roll culture.

The first photo above was taken at the opening ceremony of the 1957 festival. The other photos are of young Stilyagi, taken during the times covered in the article.

# HAIL TO THE KING – IN RUSSIA!

Elvis Presley – the King. And in Moscow on 15th June we organised a special tribute evening, to celebrate the great man.

The event was held at the Esse Jazz Café, one of the city's premier music venues. The evening kicked-off with a short introductory speech about Elvis and his life (from yours truly). This was followed by film clips of Elvis, from a year when he was in his prime – 1956.

Then, on stage, in deference to Elvis' rockabilly roots, the Hi Tones performed a great set as the climax to the evening's entertainment. I've previously reviewed the group in this magazine; they're one of the greatest rockabilly groups in Russia. Their set included Elvis numbers.

Some of those attending knew all about Elvis and came just to experience an evening dedicated to the King. But there were regular patrons of the café who didn't know all about him and it was interesting to see their reactions and responses to what was presented. Hopefully the event turned on and awakened an interest for some of these people, to Elvis and rock'n'roll in general.

Overall, it was a brilliant night. Thanks to all those who came to the support the event, especially the Hi Tones.

It's a safe bet to say that for many in our rock'n'roll community, they got turned on to rock'n'roll partly thanks to seeing and listening to Elvis. I'm talking about early Elvis; that memorable period in the 1950s when he was in his prime. In my view, the decline kicked in even before the later period of prescription drug dependence and physical deterioration. After he came out of the army, he seemed to lose a lot of that dynamic edge; still special of course, but not quite the same.

So, to conclude this article, what about the King ? The story of Elvis tastes like a very mixed cocktail, there are so many stories putting so many different slants on the man. So let's get some of the negative ones out of the way first …

The "Shine slur" was one he was never able to fully shake off. This was the allegation that in the late 1950s, when asked about the growing civil rights movement in the USA, as a white Southerner he replied, "the only good things

black people are good for, are shining my shoes and buying my records". In fairness it must be said Elvis always denied the allegation.

And of course there was the much more indisputable fact of his addiction to prescription drugs, which sadly was the main reason he never toured the UK, because of the potential consequences.

One could go on … his serial unfaithfulness to his wife while he was married, the appalling deterioration in his health and physical appearance towards the end of his life, etc. But all the above misses the central point …

Once you listen to those 1950s recordings and see the film clips of the time, they just blow you away. They are rock-solid proof he was, at his best, quite simply the greatest rocker (not just rock'n'roller) and youth icon of all time, bar none. He had everything in buckets; style, talent, looks, charisma, you name it. The word "unique" was never so appropriate as it was and is in the case of Elvis.

So here's to the King. As long as we all keep playing his music, rock'n'roll will never die.

# THE RUSSIAN "KILLER"!

This month let me introduce you to an icon of Russian rock'n'roll. They call him the Russian Killer. Those of you steeped in rock'n'roll historical knowledge will know the 1950s super star that the word "killer" conjures up in your mind. It's no coincidence …

Denis Mazhukov is a genuine legend on the music scene over here. Let me take you back to the early days …

In 1997 Jerry Lee Lewis made his debut performance in Russia, performing in Moscow. And the support act at that concert, performing before JLL came on stage, was Denis Mazhukov. Denis' style has always been hugely inspired by the Great Man, which was why he was chosen as the warm up act on this night. In a post-concert interview, Jerry Lee said, "Denis, you played just like I did when I was young."

Since then, Denis has steadily increased his big following in Russia. Not only Russia – over the years he's performed many times in the USA. Most of his USA gigs have been in New York, Memphis and Denver. And the label of the Russian Killer, inspired by the "Killer" nickname for Jerry Lee, has stayed with him. Denis' repertoire includes inspiration from other sources too. He plays many numbers in the "boogie woogie" style: He's performed at many boogie woogie music festivals in Europe over the years.

Plus he has other musical influences. One is Chuck Berry. In 1997, Denis played with Chuck Berry at the International Film Festival in Moscow. And when Berry returned to Russia a few years later, he again got Denis to play with him.

He has his own group, "Off Beat", who have been with him since he began performing in 1994. With his band he started his career playing the Moscow

clubs and as time went on the crowds got bigger and the venues more presti-gious. His repertoire of songs is huge (predictably Jerry Lee songs play a large part in his play lists). Here's some of my personal favourites that he does:

Great balls of fire, whole lotta shakin', high school confidential, roll over Beethoven, blue suede shoes and don't be cruel.

He began playing piano from the age of 6. I should add that in Russia, piano playing is much more a part of Russian culture than in the UK. More homes have pianos over here than in the West. Or at least that certainly was true at the time Denis was growing up. Interestingly his background learning as a boy was playing in the classical style. It was later as a teenager that he got the rock'n'roll bug, which then became the musical passion of his life.

Mazhukov concerts include the wildness reminiscent of the early days of Jerry Lee. Standing up, playing with the hair on his head all over the place and the occasional leg hitting the keyboards; yeah, it's the spirit of the Killer inside Mazhukov!

Take a look at this Spirit yourself: Go to youtube and type "Denis Mazhukov – the Russian King of Rock N Roll" in the search engine box. The killer is alive and kickin' – in America AND Russia!

In my article next month, I'll be covering a very special concert in Moscow dedicated to the great man himself, Jerry Lee Lewis. Stay tuned …

# THE KILLER, THE ONE AND ONLY,
# REMEMBERED IN RUSSIA

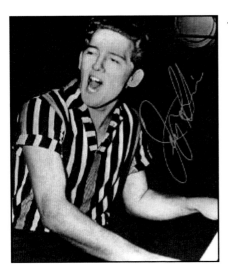

Jerry Lee Lewis, known throughout the rock'n'roll world as "the killer", has achieved a rockin' legacy that is rivaled only by that of Elvis. Some would even argue it exceeds that of the man from Tupelo, Mississippi. Thankfully Jerry Lee is still with us, albeit in rather frail health and at an advanced age.

And on 17th August we organised a special tribute evening, dedicated to Jerry Lee Lewis. The venue was the Esse Jazz Café, possibly Moscow's premier club for rock'n'roll events. The evening began with music and films of the great man, with an introductory speech on Lewis by yours truly. And then, on stage, Russia's very own "killer", Denis Mazhukov, put on a storming performance in the style of the Jerry Lee.

Regular readers of this column will know that last month I did a piece on Denis. The article detailed the inspiration Lewis had on him and about how big a name Mazhukov is in Russian rock'n'roll. Denis is known as the Russian "killer" and there was no one more appropriate to perform at this concert in honour of Jerry Lee.

Denis' performance on stage displayed many of the characteristics of the original Killer: Standing up playing the piano, the hair on his head all over the place, the occasional foot on the piano keyboard, etc. As I mentioned in last month's article, Mazhukov has his own unique style, but is heavily influenced by Lewis.

So it was a great night on 17th. And hopefully those members of the audience that night who did not know too much before about JLL, became encouraged to find out more about the legend and about rock'n'roll in general.

And to finish, what about the Great Man? From the evidence of the vast majority of people who met Lewis, 2 clear messages come out:

1. He is a rock'n'roll genius. He is unique, charismatic, colourful and untameable.
2. He is not a nice man (and that's without getting into his third marriage to his 13 year old cousin).

In a famous interview he gave in 1993, Freddie "Fingers" Lee, who met Lewis, was asked what he thought of him. His first answer was comprehensive, "a genius, an inspiration, the one and only, etc." He was then asked what he thought of him as a person. Freddie's answer was just 2 words, "a s**t".

Lewis is described as mean, selfish and arrogant by so many who knew or met him. But let's look at the other side of the coin ………….

The Great Man has given us so much joy and pleasure, both listening to his music and watching him perform. One of my favourite personal memories is going to see him at the London rock'n'roll show in 1972, at the old Wembley stadium. Leading up to the concert, there was talk of his heavy drinking and could he still cut it, etc. Well, dressed all in red he was just terrific on the night, proving to everyone present at the event that the Killer was still the one and only.

So here's to Jerry Lee Lewis. There will never be another like him. Thanks for the memories Mr Lewis and for the unforgettable music.

# CHUCK BERRY – STILL MOTORVATIN' –

# IN MOSCOW!

In the world of rock'n'roll, probably no performer has made a bigger contribution to the cause than Chuck Berry. The stories about him are legion. And here's where the Moscow connection comes in ………

In 1997 Berry made his first appearance in Moscow. There was a huge crowd to see him. Playing the keyboards and supporting him on stage that evening was Denis Mazhukov. Regular readers of this column will remember my article on Denis earlier this year; he's a real rock'n'roll icon here in Russia. And he will freely tell you the 2 biggest musical influences on him have been Jerry Lee Lewis and Chuck Berry. You can see that 1997 concert on youtube at http://www.youtube.com/watch?v=sBTLfxVoesA

And on 23rd November we organised a Chuck Berry tribute concert, which included Denis Mazhukov performing on stage. The 23/11/13 show took place at the Esse Jazz Café in Moscow. After a few words from yours truly introducing the event, it began with a film of Chuck followed by some of his

music. As usual at such events, I ran a jive dance class and all the music tracks I used were Chuck Berry classics. Then Denis Mazhukov came on stage, with his band. In my previous article on Denis, I focused on his keyboard skills. But he is also an accomplished guitarist and played many Berry songs with his guitar that night; here's just a few he did –

Sweet little rock'n'roller, Roll over Beethoven, Promised Land, Johnny B Goode, Sweet little sixteen and Schooldays.

A great night! And it was a privilege to have Denis playing for us in addition to him being the link to Berry, as the one who played with him at that 1997 concert.

Since his first Moscow concert 16 years ago, Berry has returned to Moscow more than once. His second last concert in Moscow was in February of this year. But gotta be honest, Chuck is really showing his age now and it was clear at the February event he's a shadow of his former self. For someone born in 1926, some would say he's to be congratulated for still being able to do what he does; but more of that later.

My own personal memories of Berry centre on the 1970s, when I saw him perform. The London rock'n'roll show in 1972, where he topped the bill, was unforgettable. I still remember the electrical power to the sound system conking out half way through his act. He didn't blink an eye. When the power was restored, he continued to wow us all with his rock'n'roll classics. I also remember a great concert at Hammersmith Odeon in London in the mid-70s that I hugely enjoyed: Wearing a flowery shirt, he once again gave full value for money!

Berry was a pioneer in the 1950s, along with Little Richard, in helping to bridge the racial divide with his rock'n'roll success. Although he wasn't overtly political, he is to be congratulated for his contribution in this area.

And for me, the lyrics in some of the songs he wrote rise to the level of great and wonderful poetry. For example, take time to have a look at the words to "Promised land" or "Roll over Beethoven" – you can keep your Wordsworth or Coleridge, for me Berry's poetry is the business!

As many people know, Chuck does have a mean side. His obsession with making money and arguing over the terms of concert contracts is legendary. Knowing this, it was very funny to see the February 2013 concert begin in Moscow with him arguing on stage about a written contract with the promoter, in front of a huge audience, before a song had been sung! It's on youtube at http://www.youtube.com/watch?v=rWhXhh9tdDk

He returned to Moscow again to play a concert on 20th October this year. But I took a conscious decision not to go. I had no wish to see a frail 87 year old man showing his age and clouding my truly wonderful memories, of when I saw him many years ago when he was still a sight and sound to behold. But the man's insatiable desire for dosh will no doubt keep him performing, I guess for as long as he is still able to stand up unaided. This is a shame, because at 87 he cannot "do it" any more. For example at the February 2013 concert in Moscow his performance was just embarrassing to watch.

And there's a side to him that is downright unsavoury. The most infamous case was his conviction in 1962 for transporting an under-age girl across state lines for immoral purposes. In 1979 he was again imprisoned, predictably to do with money - tax fraud. These 2 cases were not the only times he went to prison; his first period behind bars was while he was still a high school student in the 1940s (on this occasion it was for armed robbery).

But like some other rock'n'roll icons who lived a less than perfect life, Chuck should be remembered with real affection by all of us to whom he has given so much musical pleasure and great memories. As a performer and songwriter he is unique. So here's to the "Motorvator" – there'll never be another like him!

# THE GREATEST (ROCK'N'ROLL)

# SHOW ON EARTH!

This month, wanna take you back to a time before I moved to Russia. The year is 1972.

On 5th August, at the old Wembley stadium, the London Rock'n'Roll show took place. It was an epochal event, not just for those who were Teds, but for all UK fans of our great music. In my opinion, it helped towards kick-starting the 1970's rock'n'roll Revival. In other words, it was a huge event in UK rock'n'roll history.

When I arrived at the stadium, attired in my drapes and creepers, what surprised me (and many others who told me the same afterwards) was the sheer size of the crowd. We realised it wasn't just us who were crazy about our wonderful music! A magic moment early on was when we were all given the "green light" to leave the stands and go onto the pitch area of the stadium. Like Scottish football fans of bygone years, we invaded the pitch en masse, getting ourselves a birds' eye view near the stage!

The billing was a who's who of rockin' icons. But the proceedings began inauspiciously, with Heinz performing on stage. Heinz, a protégé of Joe Meek, was one of those early 1960s "pretty boy" types, who used to sing bland, poppy numbers. On stage he murdered Cochran's great hit, "C'mon everybody". Still, it was good to get him out of the way early.

Then something to behold and savour; Screaming Lord Sutch. Before he appeared, gorgeous females in bikinis carried a coffin onto the stage to the sound of raucous music. Hundreds of pigeons were released out of cages near the stage. Then Sutch appeared out of the coffin, dressed up like a were-wolf, complete with knife, hat, fake blood and make-up; brilliant! But more was to come. Between excellent rock'n'roll numbers and more outrageous antics on stage, including great dancing from the bikini clad females, the Stripper appeared. With an introduction from Sutch, she proceeded to take everyone's mind off the music (or at least for all the males present) with one of the most erotic stripteases I've ever witnessed. Errrr, not that I'm a connoisseur in these matters, you understand. Sutch's whole set was sensational and he got a thoroughly deserved standing ovation from us. And there was still Jerry Lee Lewis, Little Richard and Chuck Berry to come!

Up next was Bo Diddley. I've always liked Diddley, but never raved over his live performances. To me they were a bit one dimensional. But fair play, the guitar sound was as good as ever.

Then the Killer. Dressed all in red, Jerry Lee Lewis was high octane from first song to last. Plenty of movement, including the signature feet on the keyboards. Smokin'!

Next up, Bill Haley and the Comets; the Comets never failed to impress with the quality of their musicianship. I saw them a few times many years after 1972 and they still had it. But gotta be honest, Bill looked a little bit past his best by 1972; but still, a quality set, great to see the legends.

Then one of the biggest highlights of the show for me - Little Richard. Crazy and wild as he ever was, terrific! The culmination was his final number, "Jenny, Jenny": He ended it by jumping up onto his piano and stripping to the waist, throwing his garments to the crowd. Then he leaped into the audience, to the delight of all of us present. He'd have got my vote for being top of the bill.

But the actual top of the bill was the Chuck Berry. A fine choice. He banged out his most famous numbers, with his customary energy and movements, duck walk and all. That concert was the first time I personally heard his rude lyrics version of "reelin' and a rockin"; certainly took me by surprise! Then half way through this particular number, the electricity serving the sound system conked out! The Great Man didn't blink an eye. As soon as the power was restored he was off again, 100 rockin' miles an hour.

After Chuck, that was it - the end of a legendary concert. For me it was a privilege to have been there. My Russian rock'n'roll friends here in Moscow can only get to see such legends when they're well past their heyday, when

they come to perform in Russia. The Communist Party in charge in the Soviet Union in the 1970s would never have allowed such decadent Western culture to "corrupt" their youth!!

For those of us who were young in the 1970s and part of the rock'n'roll Revival, that concert was something very special. For some of us, it was indeed "The Greatest Show on Earth!"

# THE RETURN OF THE REEFS!

Towards the end of 2013, on 30th November, one of the biggest musical events of the year took place in Moscow. It was the return of an iconic Russian group.

The Coral Reefs (in Russian it's Korallovie Reefiy) are Russia's and Eastern Europe's greatest swing and neo-swing band. Their repertoire includes a large dose of rock'n'roll. On 17th November 2012 they performed a farewell concert in Moscow. I was at that concert and ran a dance class at the start of the show. The reason for the farewell was that the main stars of the band decided to form a new group "Via Gagry", in a new musical style. This style was very different to that of the Reefs. The best way to describe the "Gagry" sound to UK readers, is to say it's more traditionally Russian. The name Gagry is derived from the name of a popular tourist resort in the south during the years of the Soviet Union – it was a symbol of vacationing, fun and retro romance!

This past year has been a successful one for Via Gagry. Their concerts in Russia have been well attended and this new musical venture has been a big success. However, in October this year we heard the good news … The Coral Reefs were returning!

Those with good memories may remember the article I wrote in my "Russia'n'Roll" column back in the October 2012. That article described how big

the Reefs were in Russia.
Since then the line-up of
the band has undergone
change, but the essential
elements are still there.
Kir Sukhomlinov, the
band's leader and vocalist,
is still the main driving
force on stage. Mikhail
Deryabin, the only origi-
nal member of the Reefs when the group began in 1998, remains the creator
of their own compositions. After 6 years, in 2004 the musical style of the band
changed, to what we in Russia recognise as the Coral Reefs' sound today. Their
line-up features keyboards, lead guitar, bass guitar, trumpet, trombone, saxophone and drums.

I have one qualm. The fabulously beautiful Eleanora Ayrapetyan, their
former bass guitarist, is no longer in the line-up. What a shame - with her
stunning looks (as well as her instrumental skills), she added an important
element to the group. But I guess you can't have everything. The rise and
increase of more female personnel in rock'n'roll groups is an issue maybe

for a future discussion.
But long may it continue
to grow I say, especially if
they are anywhere near as
gorgeous to look at as
Eleanora!

The concert took
place at the Radio City
Club, one of the most well
known in Moscow. Once again I ran a dance class at the start of the show.
Then to a packed house (and I mean packed) on stage, it was the return of the
Reefs! Better than ever, they rocked the joint from start to finish. Plus, a pleasant surprise was a change in their style; even more rock'n'roll oriented than
before - "that'll do for me, Tommy", as Bobby Ball used to say! The vast majority of their set comprised their own compositions.

Overall it was a night to be remembered. To give you an idea of just how good the Reefs are, you can go to their web-site at www.rify.ru and click on the video link.

Welcome back to the Coral Reefs – keep on rockin' the joint, guys!

# THE ONE AND ONLY

This month let me tell you about who I think is the greatest rock'n'roll group in Russian history – in my opinion.

The group was Stressor, from the city of Tula, south of Moscow. I say was, even though the band still exists. But the one I'm talking about lasted up to 2010. Let me tell you about how great they were and then explain what happened in 2010.

The band formed in 1993 and I started going to see them after I came to live and work in Moscow in 2004. They used to come regularly to Moscow from Tula to perform. They were sensational. Their set usually comprised 2 different styles: The first half would be rock'n'roll and then after a break they'd perform a set closer to psychobilly. They'd wear different outfits for each set: The first would see them sporting sharp drape jackets, then the second they would be wearing things like prison uniforms and the like.

When I brought over Furious, the Teddy Boy group from Liverpool, to perform in Moscow in 2010, I booked Stressor to appear on the same bill. This was one of the very last ever concerts by Stressor, before the split which

occurred very soon after. The photos you can see were taken at this event.

All 4 members of the band were special. The line up was Andrey Rubliov (vocals), Taras Savchenko (guitar), Dima Bikov (contra bass), Max Kiriushkin (drums). Their performances on stage could take your breath away. The music was generally 100 miles an hour, with all 4 displaying showmanship and charisma. I have never seen a better group in any country, including the UK, in that particular style of rock'n'roll.

As I mentioned above they'd come up to Moscow from Tula on a regular basis. Their Moscow gigs were usually at the Rock'n'Roll Pub – a venue which sadly is no more. I'd make a point of trying to keep those dates free on my calendar, so I could go and watch them.

They made 3 CDs. Of the 3, my favourite was and is ""Russia'n'Roll" and yes, the name was the inspiration for the name of this humble monthly column in this great magazine! There are some tremendous tracks on this CD, most of which have Russian lyrics. It was released in 2007 on TCY Records.

The band's own prolific compositons sometimes had English lyrics, sometimes Russian: The great majority of the tracks on their CDs were their own songs. The last CD (by the original Stressor that is) was "Burn Out" released in 2008 by Crazy Love Records – another smokin' piece of work. Some of the tracks on these CDs are quite simply awesome. For example, "Surfin' Bird" on Burn Out – best version of this number ever. And "Wolfman" on the same CD, is one that can be played over and over and still give you a buzz. "Sinty Shoes" on Russia'n'Roll is similar in its impact.

They toured extensively on the continent of Europe and had a big following wherever they went. Then in the summer of 2010 came the end of the original Stressor. The group split into 2. The rift was not an amicable one. Taras Savchenko (guitar) and Dima Bikov (contra bass) left the band and formed a new group, The Magnetix. Andrey Rubliov (vocals) and Max Kiriushkin (drums) got replacements for Taras and Dima and still perform under the band's original name. Their differences leading up to the split came to a head during recording sessions in the studio, for what was meant to be their next CD. There were serious arguments between the band members during these sessions. It culminated in the break up of the group. Some of the material recorded in those sessions became the basis of the first CD released by the Magnetix, Taras' and Dima's new group.

Rock'n'Roll history teaches us that the reason for most groups breaking up is, unlike the propaganda they put out about, for example, "artistic differences", "we went as far as we could go musically", etc., etc., the real pretext was personal i.e. they couldn't stand each other any longer! However all the evidence in the Stressor split points to this one bucking this trend. The conflicts were artistic ones, to do with the way they wanted to go musically

and the role of each member in the band. For example, Taras had felt frustrated at not being given more opportunities to use his vocal skills.

What is not in contention is that the 2 groups formed out of one, the new Stressor and the Magnetix, both turned out to be top quality bands. They both still perform both inside Russia and in Europe. They are in great demand and both command big followings. They even appear on the same bills at some music festivals throughout Europe.

But nothing could be quite as great as the original Stressor. I consider myself very fortunate to have seen them in their prime. In the same way that in the 1970s I was real glad to have been able to see groups like Crazy Cavan as well as the Flying Saucers in their heyday, so it is with Stressor. And I'm talking about the 1970s Crazy Cavan and the Rhythm Rockers, not the very pale imitation of their former selves that they are today on stage. You cannot say that about Sandy Ford from the Flying Saucers today – that man still has star quality in buckets: I tried hard without success to bring him to Moscow to perform. But I am digressing from my story!

The differences between the 4 original members have healed over time. There is no animosity between them, although they don't like to talk about the details surrounding the split. I got the chance to talk to them a bit at the Moscow gigs when they were the original Stressor and all 4 impressed me as nice blokes; good characters with a sense of humour.

Catch some of the old Stressor magic yourself. Go to youtube and type in "STRESSOR - I'm Mad at You" (the Stressor official version) or "STRESSOR – Planet Zero". So I guess my column this month is a tribute and a Thank you to a group who gave so many Russian rock'n'rollers so many great memories. In my humble opinion guys, you were "simply the best".

# THE GREATEST MARCH
# IN ROCK'N'ROLL HISTORY

This month, wanna take you back to a time before I moved to live and work in Moscow. The year is 1976 and an event took place in London which has not been equaled before or since in rock'n'roll history. I know – I was there.

Despite the great rock'n'roll Revival of the 1970s, there wasn't one radio show on the BBC dedicated to rock'n'roll at that time. It was a real scandal as far as we rock'n'rollers were concerned. Especially as the BBC dominated pop music on the radio at that time – all the pirate stations had long since been banned and only a small number of independent stations, like Capitol Radio, were allowed to operate. Credit to Stuart Coleman, who was the main instigator of the campaign to get

a rock'n'roll radio show on the air. As a result of the hard work by him and others, the word went round the country amongst the rock'n'roll community that there was to be a march in London, to try and persuade the BBC to give us what we wanted. This preparatory work went on for nearly 2 years prior to the March, and it paid off – on the day the organising of the event was really excellent.

The proposed march was very much in keeping with the spirit of the times. There were many political demonstrations during that period and so the concept of a rock'n'roll demo really caught the public's imagination. A petition was also organised, which eventually garnered around 50, 000 signatures.

So the great day arrived. On 15th May 1976 thousands of rockers, mainly Teddy Boys and Girls, descended on London from all over the UK, meeting at Hyde Park for a march to BBC Broadcasting House in White City, London. What surprised many of us present, was the sheer size of the crowd. Estimates vary, but it's probably fair to say around 6,000 turned up. Amazing! A lot of us present didn't realise there were that many Teds in the country!

Unlike many of the political demonstrations of that time, the atmosphere at this event was brilliant; good natured, plenty of banter and a real sense of camaraderie. Here are just a few of my favourite memories from that day:

A really old woman wearing a Confederate uniform and carrying a Confederate flag – bizarre! The Flying Saucers on a lorry, providing us with musical accompaniment on the march – well done, guys! And that master showman, Screaming Lord Sutch, wearing a leopard skin leotard and gold coloured top hat – brilliant! Turns out, to help publicise the event Sutch had

planned to sail a piano down the Thames. But when he pushed it in, it sank! Sutch was a real one-off. What a character! I remember when I worked in north west London many years ago, I had a good friend who played in his band. One night my friend had to wait at an agreed location in Sudbury, for Sutch to pick him up to take him to a gig. My friend waited 2 hours, then gave up and went home. He found out afterwards Sutch had sacked him from the band and replaced him with someone else, but hadn't bothered to tell him. My friend only found out he'd been sacked through a third party!

In the evening, a huge concert was organised at Pickett's Lock. The stars were the Flying Saucers and Crazy Cavan, in addition to the Hell Raisers. Now here's the thing:

Having done my duty and attended the march, I missed the best fun of the day, which was the concert. At that time in my life I was very political, a real leftie. Later that day there was a big anarchist (as I remember) event and once again I felt duty called, so at the end of the march I very reluctantly left my fellow rockers and headed off for it. By all accounts the Pickett's Lock concert was excellent. One of my favourite CDs in my personal collection is "Crazy Cavan and the Rhythm Rockers at the Pickett's Lock" – a great record of a gig I wasn't at!

And the end result of all this ? Yes, the BBC gave us a rock'n'roll radio programme. Appropriately it was hosted by Stuart Coleman. But it didn't last forever. If memory serves, I think it went on for 3 years before the Beeb cut it from it's schedules. But it was worth it. This was a pivotal event in the rock-'n'roll Revival of the 1970s. It got great coverage in the mass media at the time.

Fast forward to 2014 and how many real rock'n'roll national music programmes have we got now on the BBC ? You know the answer to that, folks. Having paid the Beeb license fee all my life, up until I moved to live and work in Russia 10 years ago, after all these years it's stills frustrating, albeit less so now that I live in another country. Why has significant rock'n'roll coverage been

shunned by the BBC for so many years ? If you have your own ideas about this, why not write to the MBSN editor about it. One of my views is that rock-'n'roll is a bit too working class for the Beeb and not "trendy" enough for them.

To be fair to the Corporation, they haven't always got it wrong when it came to pop music. My generation still remembers with nostalgia the iconic "Top of the Pops" on the TV, during the period from the 60s to the 70s. That show even included a little bit of rock'n'roll now and again - for example, Matchbox and also Shakin' Stevens' "poppy" brand of r'n'r, in the 1970s. My generation will also remember the impressive "Saturday Club" on the radio at the weekends, during the same 60s / 70s period. But the lack of significant rock'n'roll on the airwaves has to rank as a blemish on the Beeb's musical history. All we were marching for back then was just one weekly radio programme playing real rock'n'roll; we weren't asking for the World!

Above all, Well Done to all those who turned up to march on 15th May 1976 – I hope some of you are, like me, still Rockin'!

# WALK ON THE WILD SIDE

This month let me take you for a walk on the wild side of rock'n'roll in Moscow. Let me introduce you to the Beat Devils.

The Devils are a 3 piece band and their style of rock'n'roll is what we'd call neo-rockabilly, somewhere between rockabilly and psychobilly. Not everyone's cup of tea I know, but I love it and there is no doubt they are exceptional at what they do. On stage, one of their distinguishing features is their sheer energy and commitment. This, combined with fine musicianship, has made them extremely popular in Russia for a long time now. They command a regular following whenever they perform in Russia. Beat Devils' concerts are a real event. Their regular crowd of followers really get into the spirit and vitality of the music and the whole thing generates a huge amount of noise and excitement.

Since the foundation of the group in 2001, their composition has changed little. And in 2004 the line-up became the same as it is now; which is Mike Bogdanov - double bass, Andy Loug – guitar and Teo Nikolaev – drums.

Although not a household name in the UK, on the continent they are well known and have toured extensively in Europe since their beginnings in 2001. They've been on many European tours both in Eastern and Western Europe. This year they have 2 more European dates still to come on their list of gigs – one in Finland, then a month later in Holland.

Loug has told me many stories about their adventures on their European visits. Here is one of my favourites:

On one of their Euro tours in 2011, in Amsterdam, when they were leaving the hotel after a show the backdoor of the car opened suddenly, and Loug's guitar slid from the car. They didn't notice it until they were almost outside the city. So they drove all the way back, and ended up being devastated as they were unable to find it. But then a local homeless man (a genuine beggar) turned up and gave them back the guitar. He'd picked it up from the floor and was keeping it for them, for when they returned! So Loug asked the poor, homeless man what he would like for this kind deed. The beggar replied by telling Loug that if he could give him 10 Euros to buy a decent beer, that would be just great! When re-telling the story, Loug always says, "my guitar is worth 10 Euros more now."

By the way, based on the band's extensive experience playing in Europe, some of you holidaying on the continent might find this information useful: Loug says, "we've played a few times in Belgium. And in the town of Mons they have the best local beer we've ever tasted!"

Most of the songs they perform are their own compositions. In addition to their high octane energy, another distinguishing feature of their songs is the quality of their lyrics - they generally have a message in them and the

quality of the writing is excellent. The creation of the songs is a real, co-operative effort between all 3 group members, although the lyrics are written by Loug. As the names of their own songs would mean little to UK readers, here's some of the cover versions they perform:

Feel So Lonely (Boppin Kids cover), Long Black Shiny Car (Mike Page, Restless cover), Whole Lotta Rosie (ACDC billy-remake), Mad at You (Batmobile cover) and Tainted Love (all-time cover). Plus they've made a few CDs. The last one was "Another dream" on Jet Noise records.

On the subject of neo-rockabilly, it's a never ending argument within rock'n'roll as to whether the genres like psycho, neo-rockabilly, etc., are part of the rock'n'roll family. Well I am not a "purist". As far as I'm concerned we're a broad church and (as long as you keep out Showaddywaddy!) we should embrace these different styles. Our Rock'n'Roll is a living, growing culture.

Have a look at the Beat Devils yourself and see what you think. Go to youtube and type in "Beat Devils @ Radio City". Or go to their web-site at www.beatdevils.ru

One final thing about the band; although you couldn't tell from the manic, frenetic style they adopt on stage, all 3 are real nice guys. There's no airs and graces about them at all, just down to earth regular blokes. So here's to the Beat Devils - satanically superb!

# THE QUASAR OF ROCK'N'ROLL!

Who is the King of Rock'n'Roll ? The answer to this question amongst rock'n'rollers is not universal, but of course most will come up with the name of the boy from Tupelo, Elvis Presley.

But not according to one of the wildest icons in r'n'r history. Little Richard claimed he was the brightest star of them all. But more of that later. On 23rd February we organised a tribute concert here in Moscow, to celebrate the legend that is Little Richard and his great music.

I began the evening with a rock'n'roll dance class. During the evening we played Richard's most famous songs. And before the band came on stage, I gave a brief speech celebrating the legend. We all gave him a big cheer and round of applause in his absence!

Then on stage, legends from Russia; the one and only Coral Reefs ("Korallovie Reefiy" in Russian), one of the most famous music bands in Russia. Regular readers of this column will know something about them from my previous articles; their style is rock'n'roll with a dose of swing. They predictably put on a superb show, rocking the joint from their first number to their last. Overall, a great evening!

Now back to the Man himself. I confess to a bias here. Little Richard was my first ever rock'n'roll hero. I thought (and still think) he was magnificent. There was also something different about Little Richard, compared to the other top iconic legends of rock'n'roll. I'm talking about Chuck Berry, Jerry Lee Lewis and Elvis Presley. In previous "Russia'n'Roll" columns in this magazine, I've documented how in their different ways these 3 legends had a dark side; in addition to detailing more importantly why they were truly Great. But Richard, in addition to being in my opinion at least equally as great, was also essentially a nice guy. And also to say eccentric would be putting it mildly; he was a real crazy banana! But the history shows he did not have the skeletons the others had.

I saw him live more than once in my youth. My biggest memory of him was at the London Rock'n'Roll

Show in 1972 (again, I wrote about this fantastic event in a previous column). For me, he should have been top of the bill that night – he was brilliant, performing "with all the brakes off"!

Film clips from the 1950s indicate he was even greater then, when he was in his prime. At that time he always seemed to be wearing suits 2 sizes too big for him with an outrageously huge pompadour on top – fantastic! I mentioned in a previous article the role of Little Richard and Chuck Berry in the 1950s, in helping to bridge the racial divide socially with their rock'n'roll successes. Although neither were overtly political, they are to be congratulated for their contribution in this area.

And it was in the 1950s, in 1957 at the height of his fame and popularity, that Richard took the most fateful decision of his life:

He quit rock'n'roll. Legend has it that while travelling on a plane in Australia during his concert tour there, the aircraft was hit by lightning. The pilot had to make a forced landing. Richard believed this was a message from God. His next step was to stand on the Sydney Harbour bridge and throw all his expensive rings (which have always been a trademark of his) away. For him this was an act of ridding himself of the devil.

Yes folks, he got religion big time. And let's face it, there are many, many worse things one can choose to do. He dedicated his life to Christianity, not only preaching but also making many gospel albums.

But he did make a comeback a few years later, albeit the music continued to take a back seat to his religion. His music became mixed with other influences, not just rock'n'roll and these were the kind of concerts I saw him perform live in. But as we say where I come from, he was still the business.

Oh yeah, one more thing about that 1972 concert …

I've heard more than one rock'n'roll purist from that time being very critical of his performance at Wembley stadium. I totally disagree. He was a bit different from the Richard of old for sure, but the outrageousness on stage only added to the act for me. But that's one other great thing about our great r'n'r culture – we can have different opinions!

Elvis is frequently referred to as "the King". During his comeback years, Richard labeled himself the "Quasar". Quasars are the brightest objects in the

Universe, so the implication was that HE was the real King of Rock'n'Roll. Many would disagree with this – but I'm not so sure.

And surely all of us can give him credit for being the original singer of the most memorable line of lyrics in r'n'r history – "A WOP-BOP-A-LOO-BOP, A-LOP-BAM-BOOM"!

Finally, all you guys and gals have been seeing and hearing a lot about Russia in the media lately. Well, here's a message from we rock'n'rollers here in Russia: We support our rockin' brothers and sisters in the Crimea and in Eastern Ukraine. We support rock'n'roll and not pro-fascist governments like the one in Kiev, Ukraine!

June 2014

# THE WILDEST CAT

Here in Moscow we rock'n'rollers revere our legends. And there are fewer more iconic than one of the wildest r'n'r cats of them all – Gene Vincent. And so on 30th March we held a tribute concert to celebrate the great man.

To complement the genius that was Vincent, we arranged for one of Russia's greatest bands, the Coral Reefs, to perform at the concert. Regular readers of this column will remember them from my articles. They're a truly brilliant band, playing great dance music with a heavy dose of rock'n'roll. The evening included video clips of Vincent at his best, plus the DJ for the evening (Dan) played many of his greatest songs. It was a wonderful night, a fitting tribute to Gene.

The story of Gene Vincent is one of the most epic in rock'n'roll history. It rises to the level of a Greek Tragedy. A performer so blessed with talent who shone like a unique bright star, who refused to look after himself (or those around him) and ended up at the end as a sad parody of his former greatness. But there were 2 years in particular, from 1956 to 1958, when he had arguably a greater period than any other rock'n'roller. Both the film clips of that time plus the music confirm this.

He was one of the artists who defined the rock'n'roll era. Along with his legendary group, the Blue Caps, he recorded some of the greatest records of the Fifties. No words written here can convey the loyalty and passion which this imperfect man stirred up in people who became lifelong devotees of his music.

In terms of his rock'n'roll career, the first pivotal moment occurred while he was still in the US Navy. He was a despatch rider and in July 1955 was involved in a collision, when another vehicle jumped a red light. He was thrown from his motor bike and sustained a severe injury to his left leg. His leg was almost severed, from just above his shin. Subsequently he didn't look after the leg properly and it developed into an even more serious disability, which was to affect the rest of his life.

The doctors treating him after the accident recommended amputation, but Vincent refused this solution. It turned out to be a bad decision and he was to live with severe pain for the rest of his life. Twice more during his life he was on the verge of agreeing to amputation of the leg, but again walked out of the hospital just prior to the planned operations. Maybe the major reason for bottling out of these subsequent operations was his belief that it would mean the end of his rock'n'roll career.

One consequence of this physical pain was his resort to alcohol and pills for relief. This only exacerbated his problems and led to rapidly declining health which killed him prematurely in 1971, at the age of 36.

Gene really hit the big time in 1956. Aided by the huge success of hit singles like "Be Bop a Lula" and "Blue Jean Bop", the legend was born. Crucial to this success during the 2 years from 1956 to 1958 was his backing group, the Blue Caps. They superbly complemented Gene's manic style on stage, with their own wild performances. Alongside the brilliant music and concerts, came the wild life style off-stage, mainly alcohol-fuelled, with wrecked hotel rooms, scandalous parties involving desirable young women, wrecked automobiles, being par for the course for Vincent and his band. During this 2 year spell, there was a big turnover of personnel in the band: Partly this was due to some of the musicians deciding they'd had enough of this physically exhausting decadent life-style. Although personally I wouldn't have minded 2 years of it!

All this high (or should I say low) life took its toll. The record company  Gene was signed to (Capitol) decided to give more of its time to the likes of Sinatra, Peggy Lee, etc., as being much safer bets. The Blue Caps disbanded after Gene refused to pay them and the American Federation of Musicians revoked his license to perform. At the end of all this, it seemed his career was kinda washed up in terms of any more stardom.

But in 1959 he was invited to perform in the UK. The instigator of this was the legendary Jack Good, and he was mainly responsible for the resurrection of Gene's career. And what a resurrection. Carefully coached by Good, Gene adopted the all-black leather look and the bad guy image on stage, to great effect. He appeared regularly on TV and headlined rock'n'roll package tours in the UK. He was once again a mega-star.

But perhaps inevitably, again things started to sour for him fairly quickly. Another pivotal event occurred in 1960, which was the car crash he was involved in. He was travelling in a cab with Eddie Cochran from a gig in Bristol to London. Tragically the great Eddie, a real rock'n'roll hero, was killed and Gene's leg was damaged still further. The loss of Cochran also personally affected him very badly. Although a bit of a wild liver himself, Eddie had been somewhat of a stable influence on Gene and had deterred him from some (not all!) of the wilder excesses from earlier days. Witnesses at the time say Cochran was more or less the only person Vincent would really listen to and take advice from.

To try and alleviate the additional searing pain he now suffered from the leg, he increased his intake of alcohol and pills. The shows he had put on in the UK up to this point had been truly memorable, but from now on they would be disappointing and a shadow of his former greatness. He also became much more cynical generally, took to carrying a gun around with him. He was involved in a number of female relationships, all of which ended in failure.

In 1968 in a hotel in Germany, Gene Vincent tried to shoot Gary Glitter. All his shots missed and the petrified Glitter fled Germany the following day. I guess in view of what we learned later about Glitter and his appalling moral behaviour, very few people will have any sympathy for Gene's target that day.

From the mid-60s until his death in 1971, Gene continued to perform but he was no longer great and these performances were testimony to the level of his decline. The cause of his death – sudden liver failure – was a further indication of how heavily he had been drinking for so long. In the period leading up to his death, he was over-weight and in very poor health, looking much older than his age. All his marriages and female relationships had failed and he died alone with little money to his name.

Those that got to know him personally during his life give mixed opinions about him as a person. Some describe him as a kind, polite individual, others give an opposite analysis of him. The consensus is that it all depended on the mood he was in and how much he'd been drinking at the time.

Interestingly, after his death he became a sort of rock'n'roll "martyr" to many rockers and is still revered by devoted fans. I can remember personally being caught up in this Gene Vincent "martyr" syndrome in the 1970s and revering him as the one and only. One can understand why – in his heyday he was truly magnificent. If ever the term "flawed genius" could be applied to a performer, it would be Gene Vincent.

So here's to the man who truly was and is still to so many a legend. As the title to one of his most famous songs bears witness, he was the ultimate "Wild Cat".

Richard Hume
Moscow

# A ROCK'N'ROLL HOME – IN RUSSIA!

This month, wanna take time out from advising you about the great Russian bands here, to tell you about an iconic venue here in Moscow:

There is a history here in Moscow of attempts to set up regular, permanent rock'n'roll venues. One of the greatest of these was the Rock'n'Roll Pub in south east Moscow. Founded by Mikhail Palitskiy, it was started shortly after I moved to Moscow in 2004, to live and work here. What a venue! At weekends it sort of became my second home, a real outpost of rock'n'roll culture here in Russia. The best Russian bands used to come and play. As I mentioned in a previous article, in my opinion the greatest of these was Stressor. They used to come up from their home town of Tula, south of Moscow, to perform there on a regular basis: Those were nights to remember! The décor of the place was also pure rock'n'roll. For example, all the framed photos and graphics on the walls were of icons like Gene Vincent, Elvis Presley, Jerry Lee Lewis, Johnny Burnette, etc. There were even some Teddy Boy graphics on the walls, thanks to material I had given to Mikhail!

Unfortunately it didn't last. The venue owners, believing they could make more money by adopting different musical styles, changed the culture and ethos of the place and the Rock'n'Roll pub was no more. Mikhail tried again at another venue, the Grease Club in central Moscow – "grease" referring to our rock'n'roll hair styles! It had a good 2 years of life with a rockin' culture, similar to the Rock'n'Roll pub. But again the owners decided to switch to another style of club and Grease, like the Pub, after a gallant life died a sorely lamented death. But a big Thank you to all those Russian

rock'n'rollers who supported these clubs, which gave us such wonderful times; above all to Mikhail, without whom it would never have happened.

This leads us on to the main topic of this article: the Rock'n'Roll events at the Esse Jazz Café in Moscow. The café is one of the most famous in the city for live jazz music. Both local and international jazz performers appear nightly at the venue. But now the café has also become a real home for regular rock'n'roll events, especially live music.

In many of my previous articles for this magazine, I've reported on concerts held at the Café and the venue has established itself as one of the premier locations for r'n'r in the city. I talked to the owner, Grant Khandzhyan, and asked him how the establishment and development of rock'n'roll at the club came about. I also tried to find (even with the assistance of his wife, Tamara!)

some juicy stories about Grant, that I could share with you in this article. Alas, Grant is the original "Mr Straight Arrow", squeaky clean with no skeletons in his cupboard. What a shame!

Q: What was the date of the first rock'n'roll concert at New Esse ?
A: The first rock'n'roll concert took place at the Esse Café in central Moscow, shortly after it opened its doors to the public in August 2011. While the first dance classes at our other Esse Café in east Moscow, if I am not mistaken, celebrated their 6th anniversary at Esse in February of this year. As I remember, the first rockin' bands to play at the Cafe were Vladimir Pankratov and Real Hot BBQ, followed by The Raw Cats.

Q: What was yours and Grant's inspiration for setting up this rock'n'roll Project ?

A: Richard Hume!

Q: How long have you been into rock'n'roll ? What were the main reasons for your getting into it ?

A: Always loved the music. And the short answer would be- to prove that rock'n'roll is alive over here! The longer one is, many circumstances coincided: I met Richard several years ago and realised that there is a community in Moscow that adores this music. All these things inspired me to start this Project at our venue.

Q: Who are your favourite rock'n'roll legends (thinking here about people like Elvis, etc.) ?

A: Apart from the great Elvis, I would name Jerry Lee Lewis and Little Richard.

Q: Who are your favourite Russian rock'n'roll groups ?

A: "The Secret" - a beat quartet, "Bravo" and " Neschastny Sluchai" were my favourite bands in 80's. I still enjoy listening to them every now and then.

Q: Why is the Café such a great venue for rock'n'roll concerts ?

A: Convenient location, close to the metro, a cosy, yet professional scene. A hall that can be fully transformed into a dance floor (we usually remove the chairs and tables for the period of these concerts). And also the audiences, comprising all the age ranges, find it more attractive to visit such places, different from the noisy, down-market and packed pubs. Although we've often had noisy and packed parties, too!

Thank you Grant, for actively helping and supporting our great rock'n'roll Culture! A Big Thanks also to his wife Tamara, who has also been active in her powerful support of Rock'n'Roll in Russia. To find out more, you can visit the Café's web-site at www.jazzesse.ru

And finally, Grant and Tamara's support of rock'n'roll is one of genuine sacrifice. As the owner of the Café, Grant makes much more money from his jazz concerts. But he runs rock'n'roll events, for considerably less money, all in the cause of supporting rock'n'roll in Russia. Nice one, mate!

All the photos were taken at the rock'n'roll events at the café. The sixth photo is one of all the staff who work at the café – Grant is the one behind the piano in the light coloured shirt on the right.

# THE FIRST ROCK'N'ROLL SUPERSTAR

Who was the first rock'n'roll star ? No, it wasn't Elvis, he came a little bit later. It was none other than the Daddy of R'n'R – Bill Haley.

On 14th June here in Moscow, we organised a tribute concert to the Great Man. To help make it extra special we booked the Russian King of Rock'n'Roll, Denis Mazhukov. Regular readers of my Russia'n'Roll articles will know about Denis. He's acknowledged as the one and only here in Russia. He's played with the best, Chuck Berry and Jerry Lee Lewis for example. If you want some proof of just how good he is, go to youtube and type in "Denis Mazhukov - The Russian King of Rock N Roll - We're Gonna Move". It's Smokin'!

The concert was a special by-invitation-only event, limited to the dancers on my Co-op Jive dance mailing list. I've already written in this great magazine about the Co-op Jive free dance co-operative, but you can find more details at www.coopjive.co.uk. As usual, at the start of the concert I ran a dance class.

Denis Mazhukov has a deep knowledge of the history of the rock'n'roll. Turns out I was glad my speech at the start of the event was brief, as Denis gave a great talk on the history of r'n'r and Bill Haley's role in it. He then proceeded to launch, with his great band, into some iconic Haley classics: "Rock around the Clock", "Mambo Rock", "See you later, Alligator", "Crazy Man Crazy" and "Shake, Rattle and Roll" – they were all there!

Overall it was a wonderful event and a fitting tribute to the the Father of Rock'n' Roll.

Bill Haley hit the big time even earlier than Elvis. It was in 1954 that he recorded, with his band the Comets, "Rock around the Clock". It can be argued this was the song that really kick-started the teenage rock'n'roll revolution. Although not the first r'n'r record ever made, it was the number that really brought rock'n'roll into the mainstream in America and then around the World. It was adopted especially by rebellious 1950s teenagers, for example the Teddy Boys in the UK, and became a sort of anthem for them.

The importance of "Rock around the Clock" can be witnessed here in Russia too. Every year in April a big concert is organised in Moscow, inviting the best r'n'r bands in Russia. The event is always advertised as Rock'n'Roll's Birthday Party i.e. celebrating the release of Haley's version of "Rock around the Clock" in April 1954. Like I said, it wasn't the first ever rock'n'roll record and the song had even been released by another artist earlier. But it was Haley's track that heralded the real birth and explosion onto the world stage of our great music. The decision by the film company MGM to use Haley's record as the opening and closing music to the film "The Blackboard Jungle" in 1955, made it even more iconic. Many teenagers at that time closely identified with the teenage characters in the film; not least the British Teddy Boys.

When Haley and the Comets toured the UK in early 1957, they took the country by storm. Most of the public were shocked by the violence witnessed at their UK concerts. Teddy Boys throughout the country, towards the end of his performances, took to ripping up cinema / theatre seats and throwing them towards the front; in other words, mayhem and rioting. One of my favourite stories is something Haley did at all his British concerts in 1957. His standard phrase at that time was, "Thank you for being such a great audience". Well, he said it at the end of all those performances in the UK, after the Teds had ripped up the seats, thrown them and generally caused fear and shock amongst the rest of the audience - "Thank you for being such a great audience"! To the Teds, Haley represented Rock'n'Roll and the culture they had adopted.

Haley was an unlikely figure to be the first rockin' superstar. He was already over 30 when he really hit the big time, a bit old to be the first teenage music idol. His background was country music and until he converted to rock'n'roll, his music was markedly different to his later classic rockin' numbers.

A crucial element in his success was his band, the Comets. Although they hardly conveyed the image of rebels, unlike for example Gene Vincent's Blue Caps, they were superb musicians and the quality of their music was clear for all to witness, even for those not into r'n'r. And hats off to the Comets: I've seen them live a few times, when they came to the UK in later years. They were quite old by then, but their sound was still superb and they have to rank as one of the best bands musically in rock'n'roll history.

I also did get to see Bill Haley himself live – once. It was at the 1972 London Rock'n'Roll Show. If you've got a good memory, you'll know I reviewed this show and Haley's performance in it, in a previous Russia'n'Roll article. He was definitely past his best by then and showing his age a bit. But the musicianship of the Comets was still excellent and it's great to be able to say I saw the legend live!

Haley had his demons. His married life was rocky and ended in divorce. He was a heavy drinker and this was reflected in his health and appearance as he got older, as well as probably being the reason for his premature death in 1981.

But he recorded some of the greatest songs in history. Even after all these years, numbers like "Rock around the Clock", "See you later, Alligator", "Shake, Rattle and Roll" and "Rip it up" are a delight to hear. If you don't believe me, spend a little time on youtube – search out those Haley classics and tell me if they still don't give the listener a real buzz. They're the epitome of rock'n'roll at it's very, very best.

Those songs, plus the vital role Bill Haley played in music history, should make us forever grateful to the man who "Razzle Dazzled" us, as much as any other rockin' icon!

# THE MONSTER RAVING

# LOONY OF ROCK'N'ROLL

This month's column is dedicated to the wildest British rocker of them all. He never had a hit record, he didn't hit the real big time like Tommy Steele and Cliff Richard. But as those of us who saw him perform and remember him at his best can testify, his contribution to rock'n'roll was immense. He was the most outrageous British rocker we've ever had.

On 19th July this year we organised here in Moscow a Tribute Concert to the great man himself, Screaming Lord Sutch. Regular readers of my column will know that tribute events to great rockin' icons are a tradition here in Russia. I myself have been involved in organising them and was glad to be able to do this one, dedicated to the memory of Lord Sutch.

In choosing a performer and a group that would be the most appropriate for such a tribute, that was easy. Valery Setkin from the Russian group the Raw Cats is the guy who in Russia gets closest to the Sutch persona. Regular readers

of my column will remember my article on the Raw Cats, which included a description of Valery's colourful history and personality. So I booked his band for the concert in July.

It was a wise choice. The event, at the Esse Café in Moscow, was a huge success. It began with me running my usual jive dance class, followed by the Raw Cats on stage; there was a great crowd and wonderful music! You can see here some of the photos taken at this concert.

His Lordship's real name was David Sutch and his greatest period musically was during the 1960s and 1970s. One of the secrets of his success was the high quality of his backing musicians, something he was careful to ensure throughout his career. And he certainly got through a lot of them. The personnel was continually changing. I mentioned in a previous article about a good friend of mine in the mid-1970s who was in his band. He waited one evening for Sutch to collect him in his car outside Sudbury station in north west London, to take him to a gig they were performing at. After waiting fruitlessly for over 2 hours my friend gave up and went home. He subsequently found out through another friend that Sutch had replaced him in the band without telling him. This was typical of his Lordship!

Another main reason for his success was his outrageous stage shows. His trademarks were outlandish costumes and themes of blood and horror. I already reported in a previous article about my seeing him at the London Rock'n'Roll Show in 1972 at

Wembley Stadium. Again there was the over-the-top costume and the fake blood, coffin, knife stabbing scene, etc. He was truly excellent at that Show, a real showman. His set included an incredible female stripper, which I also described in erotic detail in that article and will not repeat here, but will never forget!

I saw him a few times during the 1970s when he performed in London. Coming from London himself, most of his concerts took place in the capital. At least that's when he was in Britain; he spent a lot of time in the USA during this period. Every time I saw him, I was very impressed. On each occasion, he'd dress up in one of his garish costumes and perform in an outrageous style. I remember in particular one gig at the Marquee Club in London I attended – he was just sensational: Everything was "over the top'!

One of my favourites of his many costumes, was to see him dressed up as a crazed Indian Chief with hair down to his waist, with a toilet seat worn round his neck. Another was his coming on stage inside a black coffin, pretending he was locked up inside it. Other props included knives and daggers, skulls and fake dead bodies. The thing was, he couldn't really sing that well! It was his character, personality and outrageousness that made him special, in addition to the high quality of the musicians he chose to back him on stage.

He was born in Harrow and adopted the stage name "Screaming Lord Sutch, 3rd Earl of Harrow". Predictably this was shortened in time to just the first 3 words. Of course he had no aristocratic connections at all. He came from a north London working class family. I remember a Russian friend of mine earlier this year telling me how surprised he was, to find out that Sutch did not come from a titled family! One of the ideas for the stage name came from his main musical inspiration, the legendary Screaming Jay Hawkins. Those of you into rock'n'roll will know what a genius Hawkins was – a great American entertainer who could also sing brilliant rockin' numbers. The influence of Hawkins on Sutch's stage persona and style was clear for all to see.

Like I said, he never really came to close to having a hit record. But he recorded some memorable numbers. If you've never heard his version of "Jack the Ripper", check it out – it's an iconic track. Plus another favourite of mine is "London Rocker" – a crackin' number, this should be an anthem for those rockers like me from the capital. 2 others he's famous for are "Murder in the Graveyard" and "All Black and Hairy".

Sutch later became even more famous, as the founder and leader of the Monster Raving Loony Party. They stood candidates at general elections and generally enlivened and brought large doses of humour to politics in the UK. Sadly David committed suicide in 1999. Both these extra-curricular activities outside of rock'n'roll and the darker side of his private life, leading up to his committing suicide, are the two areas I'll focus more on next month in this column. One thing I can promise – the second instalment of this piece about his Lordship will be very juicy and very scandalous!

# THE MONSTER RAVING LOONY

# OF ROCK'N'ROLL – TAKE 2!

Great things are happening here in Russia, especially in the rock'n'roll world. If you believed the rubbish being said in the Western media about Russia at the moment, you probably wouldn't realise it. But take it from me, this is a great country and a great place for rock'n'roll! What a shame you are not learning the true story about Russia in the Western media, especially regarding the Ukraine.

This month am gonna continue the amazing story of Screaming Lord Sutch. You remember I began it in last month's issue and this will be the second and concluding episode about his Lordship.

In the last issue, I described a hugely successful tribute concert here in Moscow, in the great man's honour. It included some of his most famous songs

and also a live performance from the legendary Russian group the Raw Cats. This month will concentrate some more on the man's life both inside and outside of rock'n'roll, as well as detailing some of the darker sides to his character. Remember, this was a real British rock'n'roll legend to whom we should be forever grateful, especially those of us who were privileged to see him perform, in my case in the 1970s.

Sutch was a real pioneer. Already at the beginning of the 1960s he was wearing outrageously long hair before the advent of the Beatles. His garish costumes pre-dated the glam rock style over 10 years later. And his act then had shades of the psychobilly which was to emerge in the 1980s. But throughout his career he stayed loyal to rock'n'roll and made a significant contribution to our great music, especially during the 1960s and 1970s.

Some of the most enjoyable things about his Lordship are the stories about him. There were many and were usually hilarious. Here are just a couple:

In 1969 a friend of his who was a local newspaper reporter got a phone call from him, "It's Sutch here. Grab a photographer and get yourself down here. My house is on fire – it'll make a great story!" "Well, OK, David, but by the time I can get round to you the fire will be out." "No, it won't." Why not ?" "I haven't rung the Fire Brigade yet. I've got a bucket of water here – I'll wait till you arrive so you can take a shot of me pouring it over the flames." His friend got to the house 20 minutes later and to Sutch's delight, the story made the front page of the paper. Thankfully the house did not all go up in flames!

In the early 1970s, his friend the music agent Paul Barrett booked him to appear in a barn at a luxury farm in Cambridgeshire, along with Shakin' Stevens. Here's how Barrett described what happened; "All went well until Sutch decided to do 'Great Balls of Fire', featuring fire in a bucket which inevitably caught the hay in the barn alight. We saved the house, largely due to a chain of buckets – the fire brigade took ages to get there. There was much distress and many people looking for Sutch (not with the kindest of intentions). As dawn broke we were preparing to leave and I spotted a big old car parked on the edge of a field. There was a figure huddled inside, wearing a Superman T-shirt. It was Sutch. He wound down the window and enquired, "is everything alright, man ?"

His Lordship made a big impact on British rock'n'roll history, but in the UK he is much more famous for something else. In the early 1960s he set up his own political party. It stood candidates at general elections and made him a household name both at home and worldwide for a generation. The party was founded in 1963, when Sutch stood in a bye-election for the seat vacated by the former cabinet minister John Profumo. Those old enough will know of the huge scandal caused when it was revealed that Profumo was having an affair with the prostitute Christine Keeler while he was defence minister, at the same time that she was also having an affair with a Soviet agent in London. All this guaranteed tremendous publicity for Sutch when he campaigned for Profumo's vacated seat in Stratford-upon-Avon.

Of course his political campaigns were pure comedy and theatre. He christened his new party "the Monster Raving Loony Party". His campaign slogans comprised things like "I'd rather have one thousand laughs than one thousand votes," "I stand for the four Rs, reading, writing and rock'n'roll" and "vote for

the ghoul, he's no fool." He said the Party's first act if it came to power, would be to build a marble statue of Tommy Steele in Bermondsey High Street. For Sutch this approach worked: Whilst always getting only a derisory number of votes, the publicity he got was huge and he became a sort of political institution. His general attitude towards politicians and politics of "sod 'em all" resonated with the public, even if his party was too zany and ridiculous for them to vote for. In fact "Sod 'em All" was the original name of his Party!

Another event which gained him lots of publicity was his association with Cynthia Payne. For younger readers I need to quickly explain; Cynthia Payne became notorious and famous in the 1970 for running probably the most famous brothel in London, whose clientele included some of the upper class echelons of British society. She was jailed for running such an establishment. A few years after her release, she decided she too would stand as a candidate in parliamentary elections. In her case the motive was to give publicity to the campaign to change the sex laws in Britain. Anyway here's the Sutch connection – he lived for some time in Payne's house, where all these illegal shenanigans had been going on! Payne and Sutch struck up a friendship, founded originally on their common link of both being fringe parliamentary candidates.

He provided so much fun and entertainment to so many, but there was a dark side to his character. Even Payne testified to his meanness when it came to giving, especially anything involving money. Nearly all his female relationships ended unhappily. One of his most famous songs, "Jack the Ripper", had lyrics of humour and levity when describing the evil murderer. In the 1970s, those who lived through that time like myself will remember the appalling serial murders of young women, by a man who became known as the Yorkshire Ripper. During the period of the murders and before the perpetrator was caught, Sutch continued to tour the country singing his Ripper song, thinking of the extra publicity that the murders would give him. It was to put it mildly in extremely bad taste and he suffered the consequences. At some gigs, especially in the area of the country where the murders were occurring, bottles and glasses were thrown at him and he often had to make quick exits for his personal safety. It was another example of Sutch's insensitivity.

Throughout his life he suffered extreme mood swings, which included bouts of severe depression. It was while he was in such a condition that he committed suicide in 1999. But those of us who saw him perform and listened to his music have a huge amount to be thankful for. Rock'n'Roll, and in particular British r'n'r, would certainly have been the poorer without him. So here's to his Lordship, the 3rd Earl of Harrow – there'll never be another like him!

November 2014

# THE COMEDY KING OF ROCK'N'ROLL

At the time of writing this month's column, Russia is still getting a real bad press over there in the UK. And it's all Baloney. We rock'n'rollers living in Russia know the truth, which is that the people in Eastern Ukraine are fighting for their freedom. And we are with them 100%. OK, that's enough of the preaching; just wanted to let you hear the truth that you're not hearing over there in the West. Let's move on to the rock'n'roll!

Recently here in Moscow we celebrated the one and only Clown Prince of Rock'n'Roll, Screamin' Jay Hawkins. In September we organised a tribute concert at the Esse Café, to remember and enjoy the wonderful music and talent of the Great Man.

The star performer at the concert was the Russian King of Rock'n'Roll himself, Denis Mazhukov. Regular readers of this column will remember my reviews of him and some of his concerts. He is recognised over here as the country's biggest rock'n'roll star. His crazy piano style has earned him

the same nickname as that of his greatest musical inspiration, the legendary Jerry Lee Lewis – Denis is known as the Russian "Killer." We had a great night celebrating Hawkins and his music. The photo you can see of Denis was taken at the event (Denis is on the left, yours truly is in the red drapes!).

My last 2 "Russia'n'Roll" columns in this magazine told the story of Screaming Lord Sutch. Sutch's biggest musical inspiration was Hawkins and some of the greatness of Sutch can be put down to the way he performed in the style of Hawkins.

Regular readers will also probably have worked out by now that I like my rock'n'roll on the wild side. The loudness and on-the-edge nature of the best rockin' music is one of the many reasons I love rock'n'roll so much. It's another reason why it's been my chosen culture for my whole life. And they didn't come any crazier or wilder than Screamin' Jay Hawkins.

Hawkins had an interesting history even before he hit the big time musically. As a young American boxer he won the famous Golden Gloves competition, before joining the special services division of the US army, to perform his brand of entertainment at service clubs throughout the World.

On leaving the army in the early 1950s, he continued his musical career and very soon became known for his eccentric and over-the-top behaviour on stage. He would also wear exotic costumes, such as leopard-skin suits or shining gold cloaks. One of his favourite tricks was to have a coffin on stage at the start of his act. As the music started playing, he would then slowly emerge from the coffin with all the stage lights shining on him. He would also often carry a skull, which seen was smoking a cigarette, in his hand on stage; the skull even had a name, Henry!

SCREAMIN' JAY HAWKINS
COLUMBIA RECORDS

Interestingly, the legendary rock-'n'roll promoter Alan Freed was involved in helping Hawkins become famous, beginning with making sure his single "She put theWhammy on me" got lots of air play on the radio. Freed was a pioneer in promoting black artists like Hawkins, during a period when there was still lots of segregation in America. He also helped Hawkins by booking him on some of his package tours, as well as giving him parts in the rock'n'roll films he was involved in.

Jay's big break came with the release of the iconic single "I put a spell on you." The story of how this legendary record came to be cut is a famous one. Those of you who know this song will especially appreciate this story. Those that don't, check it out on youtube. It was released in 1956 and became one of the most famous rock'n'roll songs of the 1950s. The original intention was for it to be a ballad. But things changed as the entire band of musicians, as well as Hawkins,

got well and truly drunk at the recording session, with liberal quantities of alcohol being consumed at the studio. According to a music journal article written a short time afterwards, "Hawkins screamed, grunted and gurgled his way through the tune with utter drunken abandon." It was a fantastic studio recording, but Hawkins passed out after they'd finished it, completely "plastered". Afterwards he could not remember anything about the session. He had to re-learn the song from the recorded version! This off-the-wall record was unlike anything else ever recorded and sold over a million copies.

He acquired his stage nickname during the 1950s. His crazy act on stage led one young female in the audience to shout out to him, "Scream, Jay, Scream!". The "Screamin' " tag stayed with him to the end. His greatest period musically was undoubtedly in the 1950s, but he continued performing right into the 1990s and was still able to impress audiences with his outlandish act. He died in 2000 at the age of 70.

I have a great and comprehensive collection of Hawkins' records and CDs. Probably my favourite of the bunch is "Cow fingers and mosquito pie": It's a wonderful assortment of some of his finest compositions. In addition to the incomparable "I put a spell on you", the following are tracks I can also play over and over and still enjoy - "There's something wrong with you", "Yellow coat", "Little demon" and "Darling, please forgive me."

And here's a special mention of a particular Hawkins' favourite of mine; "Constipation Blues", in my opinion one of the funniest songs of all time. If you have time, check it out on youtube and see for yourself!

Like most famous musicians and performers, Hawkins lived an imperfect life. He was a notorious womaniser. All his marriages ended in divorce and when he died it was believed he had fathered around 55 illegitimate children. As time passed, it became clear the figure was closer to 75. But on stage he was magnificent. He became known as the "Clown Prince of Rock'n'Roll": There are no ifs and buts about that - he was rock'n'roll's King of Comedy!

December 2014

# DANCE TO THE GUITAR MAN

This month wanna introduce you to a real Russian rock'n'roll icon. He's one of the most famous guitarists in Russia and has been on the r'n'r scene for nearly 30 years.

He's Oleg Ivanin and is most famous for his role as lead guitarist for the one and only Great Pretenders, one of the greatest Rockabilly bands in Russian history. He's played in other groups too and still does. I interviewed him recently to find out more about his illustrious career as well more about the history of Russian rock'n'roll through his own personal experiences.

I believe my summary of the interview (below) will help give you more of

an insight, not only about Oleg, but into the history of Russian rock'n'roll.

I began by asking him when and why he first got into rock'n'roll. He advised he'd always enjoyed this style of music and began his career as a guitarist in 1987 playing in an independent rock band named 'Meeting On The Elbe'. The Band was successful, he joined the 'Moscow Rock Laboratory' (an organisation which united the best rock bands of that time), planned to release their first album, etc. They had one number called 'Meeting On The Elbe' – it was the first rock'n'roll song he ever performed. He realised in hindsight that he played the song too "jazzily"! In 1988 due to disagreements with the leader of the group (who wanted to play more pop music) he left the band and was invited to join another group called 'That's All Right, Mama'. This band played rockabilly and their vocalist, Oleg claims, had a voice similar to Elvis Presley and looked almost like Mick Jagger! The bass guitar player was an old friend of his whom he hadn't seen for 9 years, so that was a nice surprise for him.

I asked Oleg who were the big names in Russian rock'n'roll when he began his rock'n'roll career. He recalled a few performers; Pete Anderson, 'Mister Twister' and Denis Mazhukov's 'Off Beat'.

I already knew about Anderson's legendary status in Soviet rock'n'roll. For sure, the name Pete Anderson does not sound very "Soviet" – it's the name he adopted for himself. Under Communism, Western radio broadcasts were often "jammed" and Western rock music was discouraged through varying degrees of censorship, as well as being criticised in the communist controlled media. Music records and books brought in by travellers from the West were often confiscated at the borders. But through all this, pioneers like Anderson continued to perform and play rock'n'roll.

Here's a true story about him, with a UK link:
In a previous Russia'n'Roll article, I did a piece on the London Rock'nRoll Show in 1972. It was an iconic event in British r'n'r. All the big names performed at the Show, Chuck Berry, Jerry Lee Lewis, Little Richard, Bill Haley, you name it they were all there. So was I! Well, full credit to the organisers of the event, they also invited Pete Anderson to perform at the Event. It would have been a momentous happening. As I mentioned, in 1972 in the Soviet Union examples of western culture like rock'n'roll were officially discouraged and cracked down on. So the fact that Anderson had had the guts to openly adopt and play rock'n'roll was commendable. Plus he was a really good performer. But here's what happened. On hearing of this official invitation to Pete to perform in London in 1972 at such a prestigious and public event, the Com-

munist authorities banned him from leaving the country to attend it, so the momentous happening never happened. Anderson still has the official invitation letter from the show organisers, framed and displayed in his house! Anyway, well done Pete, you were one

of the pioneers who kept the flag flying for rock'n'roll behind the Iron Curtain in those early days.

Of the other 2 names Oleg mentioned above, Mister Twister and Denis Mazhukov, both are still performing after all these years. Mister Twister are not quite the power-house they were in those early days, but Mazhukov sure is. I've already written about him in "Russia'n'Roll" – he's the king of Russian rock'n'roll!

I asked Oleg what he thought were some of the most important events in Russian r'n'r history. He referred again to the importance of the Moscow Rock Laboratory that organised concerts in the late 1980s, which enabled bands to become popular in Russia. The Laboratory played a key part in developing and popularising the music.

Oleg is a good friend of mine and, not during this particular interview but a few years back, told me something about the early 1990s in Russia after the fall of Communism. At that time the antics of what can only be described as real gangsters were much more prevalent than they were before or since. Here are some facts:

Some members of bands were killed by gangsters in shoot-outs, one was even killed on stage. This lawlessness was not confined to the music business but was part of society generally for that brief period. Things settled down and now such outrages are a thing of the past (with very very few exceptions). But those who lived through those times understandably haven't forgotten. My response when Oleg told me this was - Thank goodness for Vladimir Putin and law and order!

About the changes in Russian rock'n'roll over the years, Oleg's analysis is that the repertoire hasn't changed much, but the quality of the performances has, drastically, due to better commands of the instruments (some Russian rock'n'roll guitarists of the 1980s and early 90s made too many mistakes during the gigs, irritating the audiences). The quality of the sound is much better now, due to good musical instruments being available nowadays in Russia. There are good reasons for this: It was very difficult to buy a professional guitar in the 1980s in the Soviet Union and was extremely expensive – prices for American guitars were comparable to the prices of new cars back then. And it was difficult enough to buy a car in the Soviet Union even if you did have enough money. So Oleg's conclusion is that the advent of Capitalism has been good for Russian rock'n'roll!

I was particularly interested in Oleg's role in the Great Pretenders. I'm a big fan of the group and have been following them during the 10 plus years plus I've been in Moscow. I asked him what were the reasons for their success and their longevity. Oleg's assessment is that their repertoire is good – they cover only one version of each song, sorting through dozens of options, plus they play their own stuff, trying to be diverse. He said they've been performing for such a long time because they "like to play this wonderful and positive music and just cannot stop doing it!"

I was hoping to get some juicy anecdotes from him about personal differences between members of the Pretenders over the years, so asked him if there had been any difficult periods for the band in this area. Alas, he replied they'd been lucky so far, all members of the group have always been nice guys. What a shame! But he was able to provide me some amusing anecdotes about his history of working with double bass players with the Pretenders. Here they are, as told by Oleg:

"We had difficulties obtaining double bass players, due to the general shortage of such musicians on the rock'n'roll scene. So we asked one guy to play with us at the gig. He played well but the stand under the strings of the instrument jumped out so he had to stop to fix it, then he calmly tuned the bass and continued to play very confidently but .... played the wrong part of the song. After several minutes all this was repeated, then it happened again and again. I was in shock but the audience was excited, thinking that it was part of the show!

Shortly after that we found another bassist and invited him to the rehearsal before a gig. And he disappeared! It was minus 27 Celsius in Moscow and we were very nervous for him. He arrived almost at midnight with a double bass split into parts. We had to perform the next day! Everybody was in shock. But he managed to glue the instrument together and played quite well. Richard, it was Vadim, you remember him maybe ? [yup, I do!] So the Great Pretenders have always had great adventures with their bassists."

And here's another one from Oleg worth a listen. It doesn't involve the Great Pretenders, but does include another bass player:

"In the mid-1990s I had my own project where we played instrumental numbers composed by me, plus pop, rock and rock'n'roll covers. Our drummer was a very famous musician but on one occasion he got fed up waiting for the beginning of the gig. So he entertained himself along with the bassist for an hour or so with two large bottles of vodka and two apples. We performed a very fast song 'Wild Little Willie' and couldn't stop because the drummer continued to play, though he used to tell me that he was too old to play fast numbers! After five unsuccessful attempts we finally stopped. Our vocalist said to me afterwards that it was a shame and he had never been so upset at a gig before. However my friends came to me after the concert and told me excitedly that the best part of the show was the number where we couldn't stop! Nobody was aware that this part of the show had been directed by alcohol!"

Of his rock'n'roll heroes, Oleg again referred back to Pete Anderson. Oleg's biggest musical inluences ? "Chuck Berry, Shakin' Stevens, Bill Haley, Gene Vincent, Brian Setzer". All time favourite rock'n'roll performers ? "Elvis Presley, Brian Setzer". All time favourite song ? - "These Boots Are Made For Walking".

Oleg is optimistic about the future of rock'n'roll in Russia, because he says so many people in Russia don't know the music yet. Many friends of his often tell him after the concerts that they couldn't even imagine beforehand how great rock'n'roll is! He says "the music is easy to perceive, energetic, very positive – almost everybody likes it."

The photos you can see comprise the interviewee and the interviewer, plus Oleg performing with the Great Pretenders.

Thank you to Oleg for a quality interview. Keep playin' the Great Music, mate!

# THE UK ROCKABILLY RAVE –

# RUSSIAN STYLE!

This month wanna cover a real big event in the UK this year, with a Russian flavour. At this year's Rockabilly Rave in June, at Camber Sands, one of Russia's finest all-time bands, the Hi Tones, came over from Moscow to perform.

All the feedback received indicates they went down a storm. It certainly didn't surprise me, since I've been seeing them perform since the inception of the band in 2010. Regular readers of this column will know I did an article about them last year, in addition to doing a review of their CD "I'm gonna leave you" on Sam Records, for this magazine. They're simply excellent, real raw rockabilly played and performed in the authentic 1950's style.

They comprise a lead guitar, acoustic guitar, upright bass and drums. They've become hugely popular on the rock'n'roll scene in Russia, particularly amongst the followers of rockabilly. Their leader is vocalist and acoustic guitarist Alexey Schukin. He founded the group in 2010 with the aim of playing authentic 50's music. Alexey says their musical inspiration comes from the likes

of Johnny Burnett, the Delta Bombers, Eddy and the Backfires and the Rhythm Shakers.

They were not the first Russian group to appear at the Rave. A few years back, the Neva River Rockets from St Petersburg performed there. And in more recent times, the Moscow band Diamond Hand also performed at the event. But the Hi Tones rank much higher in terms of quality and status in Russian rock'n'roll. The Rockets, to use a football metaphor, were strictly second division. Diamond Hand do qualify as a premier league group, albeit a bit conservative in their style.

The photos of the Hi Tones you can see comprise one taken at the Rockabilly Rave and some at their concert in Moscow at the Esse Café on 15th November.

I arranged to interview band leader Alexey Schukin, to ask him his impressions of the Rave and about the UK. I should add here Alexey is a man of few words who is not given to interviews. He is also blunt and to the point with some of his answers to questions. He kindly agreed to my interview and here's the result:

I asked him why they went down a storm at the Rave and his response was classic Alexey: "The main reason for this is that we are a really cool band. That's why." He saves his best performances for the stage, not for interviews! I asked him

what things he liked best about the Rave, expecting a long list of great performances, but his answer was unusual; "Huge feathered birds, that were walking all over the festival grounds." How many of you attending the Rave can remember these birds ? I hope someone at the festival performed "Bird is the

Word" just for these extra customers. But Alex did tell me which performer impressed him the most; "John Luis. He is our friend and he's the Best."

He was complimentary about the UK rock'n'roll scene, based on the band's brief visit: "I was really impressed that r'n'r life in the UK is very rich and varied. There are lots of people who like this music, plenty of olds cars and motorcycles; and young women – good looking, nice and stylishly dressed." I've lived and worked in the UK, the USA as well as Russia and in my opinion there is no question Russian women are the best looking in the World. So as a Russian Alex's observation of the young female British women at the Rave is praise indeed! As for me, my vote still goes to the Russian women!

He found the Brits to be very friendly during the visit, but said there was no curiosity amongst them about Russia. I asked him if anyone asked them about the current happenings in the Ukraine and he replied that he doubted that many of them knew anything about it at all. Now that's encouraging, it means all the anti-Russian propaganda presently being gurged out in the mainstream Western media is clearly not having a great effect on a large number of people.

Alex singled out Jerry Chatabox, the festival organizer, to say a big Thank you to him for the way they were treated and looked after during their stay: "We were really impressed by his hospitality and warm welcome."

He said the most surprising thing about the whole adventure happened at the end: "All the festival was exciting, but the most surprising was that our drummer had to go to the hospital when he got back to Moscow, because of the amount of alcohol he had drunk at the Rave."

The Hi Tones continue to go from strength to strength. They have a new album shortly to be released on Wild Records in Los Angeles. In April next

year they will take part in the Viva Las Vegas festival; "somewhere in the Nevada desert" as described by Alexey.

My final question was to ask him what he thought of our rock'n'roll scene here in Russia right now. He gave me an answer which I cannot repeat in a family magazine like this one! Aleksey's opinion of the r'n'r scene differs markedly from my own and from the great majority of Russian rock'n'rollers. Like I said, he is generally a man of few words, which are usually blunt and to the point!

If you weren't at the Rave, you can have a look for yourself on youtube to see how great the Hi Tones were at the Festival. In the search engine box, type in "Hi Tones rockabilly rave 2014". For those who were at the Rave, it was an excellent opportunity to see an example of just how good the rockin' bands are over here in Moscow. And the Rave organisers made a great choice in selecting the Hi Tones to represent Russia!

# THE MOVIE THAT ROCKED BRITAIN

This month I wanna take time out from telling you about the great things going on in the rockin' World here in Russia, to take you back to an iconic event in rock'n'roll history. Here in Moscow we organised a special concert to commemorate its anniversary.

In 1956 the first ever rock'n'roll film was made. "Rock around the Clock" was a Columbia Pictures production which was released in the UK later that same year. On 6th December at the Esse Cafe in Moscow I organised, along with the venue owners, a concert to celebrate the film's UK release all those years ago. Our Moscow event included showing some clips from the movie. The real stars of the concert were the Raw Cats, performing live on stage. Regular readers of this column will remember them, from my glowing comments about them in previous issues. In particular, their leader, keyboards and vocalist, is a Russian rockin' legend. They are a fantastic group specialising in 1950s' style rock'n'roll, so there was no better choice to help us pay tribute to

the great film. We had a great 1950s' style night in Moscow! You can see here some of the photos we took at the concert.

Why celebrate a film in this way? The following is the story of why the movie was so significant in r'n'r history, especially in Britain.

In the mid-fifties there was a real social (not political) revolution going on. For the first time, an independent youth culture had sprung up in the West. Central to this was the music, Rock'n'Roll. And the movie was one the youth were able to totally identify with. The most significant content in the film were the songs performed. There were many and here are some of the most notable - "Rock around the Clock", "See you later Alligator" and "Razzle Dazzle" by Bill Haley and the Comets; "Teach You to Rock" and "Giddy up a Ding Dong" by Freddie Bell and the Bell Boys; "Only You" by the Platters. These were historic rock'n'roll numbers and for the audiences, seeing these groups perform them in the movie, it made a huge impact.

And this impact was a surprise to nearly everyone. It was only released as a "B' movie on a small budget. But it was the timing of the movie that made all the difference, right at the start of this "social revolution" I mentioned above. Teenagers at the time went crazy over it. Suffice to say it caused a tremendous response. Most youngsters loved it, whilst many older people saw it as symptomatic of all that was wrong with the new generation.

I first saw the film in the 1970s as a young Teddy Boy. I thought it was brilliant. When watching it, one needs to always keep in mind the time it was made. Some of the dialogue now might seem a bit dated, old fashioned and even tame by today's standards. But back in the 1950s it was, well, revolutionary in it's challenging of the established Music Order. Although some of the script in the movie was decidedly "middle class American", the working class youth in the UK really related to the new musical culture and style on show in the film. This was especially true for the Teddy Boys and Girls.

Following the release of the film in 1956 in the UK, the mayhem and disorder it caused made headlines in the national media. Above all it was the Teddy Boys and Girls causing all the trouble. Newspapers, local and national, reported on the riots throughout the country, especially inside the cinemas where the movie was being shown. Cinema seats were slashed, there were fights between Teddy Boy gangs and the police, you name it! These are some of the headlines from the newspapers at the time:

"Rock'n'Roll mayhem: 400 riot in cinema", "Wild mob rock'n'roll into street after cinema riot", "Raving youths fined after rock'n'roll film", "Rock'n'roll film

has police standing by for riots", "1,000 rock'n'roll rioters take city by storm" and "Rock'n'roll frenzy brings out police". To give you an idea how serious these riots were, here's the beginning of a headline article from the Daily Herald, a national newspaper at the time; "Teddy Boy 'Rock" Riot Again – Usherettes trampled – Rock'n'roll crazed rioting – the worst yet – broke out again this afternoon at the Caiety Cinema, in Peter Street, Manchester, where the film 'Rock around the Clock' is being shown. A gang of 100 youths stormed down from the balcony to the stalls, seized hosepipes and sprayed the audience. Lighted cigarette butts were thrown from the balcony. A stool also went over. Armed with broken pieces of the stool, youths struggled with police. Light bulbs were snatched down and thrown into the fray. Usherettes were thrust aside and trampled. One was struck on the leg by an exploding bulb."

This violence was of course indefensible. But it gives an indication of the intensity of this "social revolution" I spoke about above. Britain had seen nothing like this before amongst their younger generation.

Remarkably, if you watch the film you'll see there is no real violence in it to speak of. The film had a "U" rating i.e. anyone including children can view it. It tells the story of how rock'n'roll was discovered. It is a very fictionalised account, but very entertaining nonetheless. Some of the highlights are the performances of Bill Haley and the Comets, plus some great jive dance sequences. There is even an appearance by Alan Freed, playing himself. Many of you will know Freed's huge contribution to the birth of rock'n'roll as a promoter, albeit he ended up being disgraced for taking payments for illegally publicising certain records: But that's another story. In 1956 the film was also ahead of its time in the USA in terms of social progress, in that it showed white musicians performing in the same venues as Black performers.

So this is a story of a low budget B movie that rocked the World. If you haven't seen it yet, check it out. It's a wonderful slice of rock'n'roll history.

# SWEET AND HOT – TAKE TWO!

Quite some time ago, I did a piece in this column on a fantastic group here in Moscow. The column was entitled "Sweet and Hot!" Well, here we are second time around:

The group are the Marshmallows, 3 beautiful young Russian female singers, who perform excellent 50's style rock'n'roll. They're brilliant. They're a real phenomenon on the rockin' scene here. They are supported by 3 musicians, guitar, bassist and drummer. Since my last article on them, the band have gone from strength to strength. There has recently been a small change to the line-up - Masha Nosova and Yulia Chugueva remain but Nadezhda Kunareva has been replaced by Olya Korovina.

The photos you can see were all taken at their concert at the Esse Café in Moscow on 10th January. I decided in view of their success and progress following my last article on them, it was time to talk again. So after the concert, which I organised along with a rock'n'roll dance class I ran to start the event,

I sat down with the 3 beautiful women, to ask them about all things Marshmallows. Here is the result – the story of the group and more, as told by the band themselves. As a very recent newcomer to the trio, Olya left the talking to Yulia and Masha.

They began by telling me how they got into rock'n'roll. Julia said she grew up with the music: "At the movies and on the radio I was captivated by it and as I grew up I got 'married' to rock'n'roll and my whole life was consumed by it." Masha said before she first met Yulia and started singing with her, "I listened to everything rock'n'roll – this is the music of carefree youth and so you meet a lot of 'positively charged' people, because they'll always be young."

And how did the Marshmallows come about ? Yulia provided the initial spark for the genesis; "the idea came to me when I sang in a choir (this studio catered to girls). At first I was thinking about a solo program, but while I was in the choir I started thinking about polyphony (a trio), the kind of thing that was popular in the 1950s". Masha said that fitted her profile too, "before singing in the same choir as Yulia, I sang in a quartet where we did our own arrangements." It snowballed from there. Yulia said her choir teacher supported the idea and worked with them on the programme. They didn't expect the first Marshmallows shows just a few months later to be so compelling. Yulia said they generated a lot of interest, "things really took off, surpassing our expectations."

Musical influences ? Yulia first of all drew attention to the impact the Raw Cats had on them. I've written already in this column about the iconic status of this group in Russian rock'n'roll, especially their leader vocalist/keyboard player Valery Setkin. Yulia said their first ever show happened because of the

Raw Cats. "They helped us to believe in ourselves, overcome our stage fright and to take the lead role. We just sang for their friends, gradually getting used to the stage, microphones and audiences, while continuing to work on our own programme. After 6 months we did a show for the Raw Cats' birthday."

Masha says the American groups of the 1950s were their point of reference; "they had a style that was somehow unique, since for the most part women's vocal trios in Russia sing jazz, that's what they know more about. Our project says things no one else is saying."

About the important events in the history of the Marshmallows, they say every one of their concerts is an event and it's hard to say which of them is more important, "there are always new people and loyal fans, and every time we do a show we create the mood and atmosphere of the 50s era, or at least we try." Masha remembers their first open air concert at Kuznetsky Bridge in Moscow, "performing on the street in front of a big crowd of people just walking by – this was new and very, very exciting!"

Yulia says the public in Moscow tend to respond to things generally in a way that is "very cold, because of the climate apparently, and it's pretty difficult  waiting for them to respond to the words and music, since for them this is something new and unusual in today's musical milieu." I've been here in Russia for over 10 years and that's not my impression: If Russians like something, they are very open in expressing it. And at all the many Marshmallows concerts I've been to, the audience has been to say the least very very appreciative and responsive.

I asked them about changes on the rockin' scene here in Russia. Yulia said there were less clubs than there used to be, "a lot of clubs have closed, including the ones we first began performing in. There aren't many public squares where large groups like ours can play, since there are six of us (including the musicians), and our style isn't suitable for many venues. We hope that by now (we've been performing for 3 years) the audience has learned more about this music and about that point in time when the whole world experienced a music revolution." You said it, Yulia - the 1950s, unlike all the stuff that came after, really was a social revolution. For the first time, the youth adopted their own music, culture and lifestyle, unlike previous generations. All the movements that came afterwards, mods, rockers, punks, skinheads, glam rock, etc., were just a continuation of this. Masha pointed out the rising popularity of Rocka- billy and Psychobilly in Russia, "although perhaps only in certain areas. We don't limit ourselves to the 'party scene' and we try to perform for anyone who likes what we do, and there are many."

Reasons for their great success here in Russia ? Masha says it's down first of all to good old-fashioned "constant hard work. We understand that the au- dience appreciates more than a pretty picture – they also want a quality per- formance, so we are constantly rehearsing, both together and on our own." For Yulia, "what's important is that the picture be complete, so we pay a lot of attention to details, from creating the image of 'the girls from the pictures,' to the sound of the instruments and voices, because the audience isn't fooled; they can see and hear what is fake."

Apart from Olya replacing Nadezhda, as advised above, the line-up of the singers hasn't changed since their foundation. But there has been a big turnover of backing musicians. "Many times we've changed musicians", they

advised me, "also, it's hard to find a good guitarist for this genre and even more so on a regular basis. Our main prob- lem has always been the rhythm section and only a year ago we found some fellows who played our sound almost perfectly. We're glad we found them! They are Vladimir Kondrashov (bass) and Sergey Arnautov (drummer). We hope for long and fruitful work with them."

I asked them for some funny or particularly interesting stories about the group. Here's the result: Yulia – "Once we

were invited to play one of the largest video game exhibitions in Russia. It was funny because there was a large stage and an auditorium with everything. We and the organisers put a lot of work into it. But we didn't perform, the explanation being that we were too loud!"

Masha – "Yes. And it can happen that we end up performing only as models for photo shoots. For example, one time there was this festival for vintage cars. A year later, in one of the magazines, in an announcement for the same festival there was our photo from a year earlier. That was nice. And once there was this guy who jumped onto the stage with us during the song and asked us to stand next to him, saying 'what you have here is such fun and beautiful'."

Masha and Yulia quoted the names of individuals in the history of Russian rock'n'roll that they particularly admire, for their contribution to the rockin' scene here in Russia; "The Raw Cats (especially Valery Setkin), the Hi-Tones, Aleksey Lex Blokhin, Denis Mazhukov, Yevgeniy Kudryashov, too many to remember, but all of them are important in their own way and they did a lot for rock'n'roll in Russia."

They count their biggest musical influences as being the Boswell Sisters and the Andrew Sisters. Now, most of you know about the Andrews Sisters, but if you haven't heard of the Boswell Sisters, check 'em out on youtube: They're an amazing slice of twentieth century music history.

All-time favorite rock'n'roll performers ? Yulia – "for me, Wanda Jackson and Janis Martin." Masha – "for me, of all the rock'n'rollers, Chuck Berry and

Jerry Lee Louis will always be in first place." And in answer to my serious question, "if someone put a gun to your head and told you to say your all-time favourite track ? ....... Yulia – "Bang Bang by Janis Martin!" ...... Masha – "Bang Bang by Nance Sinatra!"

Regarding the future, "our group is doing all it can to ensure that rock-'n'roll will have a future in Russia." Masha - "I see us on a large stage with an orchestra, everything is glittering and sparkling, it's filled with people and everyone is there to see us!" Julia – "Of course, sooner or later we'll conquer the word. But seriously, we will continue to celebrate rock'n'roll in our Marshmallow Universe."

Catch some of the Marshmallows' magic yourself. You can see them on Facebook – type "Marshmallows" in the facebook search engine box. Like I said, "Sweet and Hot"!

# A ROCK'N'ROLL LIFE

Rock'n'Roll is not just about the super star performers and the legends. Of course they're important to us. But many of us have a rock'n'roll story of our own, of how we first got into the culture and how it has influenced our lives. For example, how did you first get into rock'n'roll, dear Reader ? Bits of my own story you've read about in passing, in some of the articles I've written in this column for nearly 3 years now.

This month you're going to hear about one of those stories, not mine but it is also someone who has well and truly lived the rock'n'roll life. Dmitry Vinogradov is a well established icon on the scene here in Russia. His r'n'r history goes back a long way. He knows all the rockin' stars in Russia and they know him. When I first came to Russia in 2004, it became clear to me early on how high his reputation is on the rockin' scene here. Here is his story below, in his own words. It will tell you not just about him, but also about Russian r'n'r history. The photos you can see go back to the 1990s and are snapshots of Dmitry's rock'n'roll life.

"Hi, Richard! I'm going to start trying to reply to the questions you've asked me. I've been listening to rock'n'roll for as long as I can remember. My

father was a great admirer of Elvis, Chubby Checker, and Bill Haley, so I started listening to this music when I was still a child growing up in Moscow, although not entirely consciously. I wasn't interested in music at all until I was 13 or 14. It somehow fell outside of my range of interests at the time. But then, things started happening. Firstly, Bravo with Zhanna Aguzarova." At this point in Dmitry's story I need to step in and explain about Bravo. They had a huge influence on Russian rock'n'roll. They were founded in 1983 and their style was primarily 1950s r'n'r. In the 1980s they were real super stars in Russia, which had a lot to do with their lead singer Zhanna Aguzarova. She had everything, looks, charisma and a great voice. But she left the group in 1988 and as a result the group's enormous following waned. They were still popular and attracted big crowds, but not on the same scale as before. Here's Dmitry continuing the story of Bravo:

"Incidentally, I was 14 when I first saw and heard them. For 2 more years, I wasn't particularly interested in them – I liked them, but that was all. And then I began to understand – this is my thing! I started dressing like them and listening to their songs. I had just seen Angel Heart with Mickey Rourke and had become a big fan of the 1950s style. Around the same time I saw Mister Twister on TV" (this was another famous rockin' band of the time in Moscow. They are still going strong, albeit nowhere near as popular as they were in the 1980s). "In the 1980s I began going to rock'n'roll concerts – I saw Bravo first and then Mister Twister. And here I am, I have been partying ever since! Things just happened like that.

Regarding the best Russian bands of the 1990s, well my opinion is biased – whoever I've seen live are the best for me. In the early 1990s I saw Bravo, then Off Beat, the Alligators, Mister Twister, the Jailbreakers, Crazy Man Crazy and Steam Engine. Many of the bands appeared, then disappeared, then resurfaced again. The groups from St. Petersburg always impressed me. About the very best ones, well most often we went to see Denis Mazhukov and his group

Off Beat". (Again, dear readers, if you have a good memory you will know from my articles in this magazine of the iconic status of Denis Mazhukov, 'the King of Russian Rock'n'Roll'. Carry on, Dmitry) "Denis is the Russian Jerry Lee Lewis! This was around 1994-96. There were many bands. To be honest, I don't remember all of them now. The most important thing for me has always been to be able to dance to the music. This is how I judge the best bands.

Who's the most prominent rock'n'roll musician in Russia ? It's very hard to talk about one particular person, the rest might just get offended! After all, I'm friends with all of them. Like I said, if I feel like dancing to a given band's music, that one is the best for me. But I guess if I had to choose one group from the above it would be Denis Mazhukov and his group Off Beat. Why did I always go to watch them and considered them to be the best? The answer is all about dancing! Denis clearly understood rhythm and to move to him was very easy and simple! In general they were excellent - they played profession-ally and cheerfully and they put on a great show.

If I had to choose the most prominent rock'n'roll musician in the world, for me it would be Bill Haley. Of course I started with Elvis, but to me Bill is closer with regard to the music, because he's always been easy and pleasant to

dance to. In 1992 I started danc-ing jive, and with my first train-ing tutorial there was a video with a clip from the film 'Rock around the Clock'. The whole video was 40 minutes long, no more, just musical numbers and dance scenes. For those wishing to learn how to dance in Russia at that time, this was a must. I probably watched this tape 500 times! Since then, for me Haley is No. 1 in Rock'n'Roll!

The times were fun. The 1990s in Russia were crazy! In the good sense. It was the time of our rock'n'roll revival, a time of hope. And overall, those who say they remember all those times in the 90s didn't live in the 90s, because alcohol was a very important part of all our shindigs and as a result none of us remembered everything!

As for appearance i.e. the clothes we wore, well in the 80s (and the early 90s) we wore clothes that we could buy at Tishinsky Market - a well-known Moscow flea market, torn down in the late 90s. There it was possible to buy practically any sort of clothing

and footwear from the 1940s up to the 1980s. We nicknamed this apparel 'Tishka' or 'Tishinka' in reference to the name of the market. For the most part, these were products of the USSR, but there were also foreign items. Everything was in varying degrees of preservation, but it was possible to find good stuff if you really wanted to. But then in 92-93, I wanted something more; I wanted to wear things specially tailored for me. In Moscow there were several tailors where it was possible to get something made for you 'a la Teddy Boy', especially drape jackets. You just had to explain to the tailor what you wanted from him beforehand - and this wasn't easy in those days! Well in Moscow there then opened a shop called 'Marley of London'. They were supposed to cater for the mod style, but in fact the bulk of their stuff was black leather jackets and cowboy boots. The young women dressed more simply - pin-ups were practically unseen; in general they wore either jeans and black leather jackets or old dresses from 'Tishka'."

Thank you to Dmitry for a great insight into his r'n'r story and above all about Russian rock'n'roll history. It's a great history, filled with many rockin' heroes like Dmitry!

# SOMETHIN' ELSE

In Moscow on 14th March I was pleased to host another tribute concert, to a great rockin' icon. The artist in question this time can well and truly be said to have conformed to the culture of "live hard, die young." His name was Eddie Cochran and he was one of the greatest rock'n'rollers of all time, despite the fact he died at the age of only 21.

Regular readers of this column will know I organise rock'n'roll concerts on a regular basis in Russia. On 14th March I held a concert at the Esse Café in Moscow, to remember the great man. The Café is an iconic venue for rock-'n'roll in Moscow. I booked the Great Pretenders to perform at the event.

Readers of this column will remember my piece on them; they are a superb rockabilly band with a great rock'n'roll history in Russia. They were a fitting choice to celebrate the legend of Eddie Cochran. A great night was had by all. You can see here some of the photos taken on 14th.

Cochran composed and performed some of the most famous rockin' songs of all time. For example just look at this list of numbers – "C'mon everybody", "Teenage heaven", "Three steps to heaven", "Twenty flight rock", "Somethin' Else" and the immortal "Summertime Blues". A while back, I compiled a "Top Ten rock'n'roll tracks" for this magazine. I put Summertime Blues as my all-time number one and I haven't changed my mind. The only amendment I'd make to that Top Ten today, would be to add Eddie's "Somethin' Else" to it.

Another very special quality about him was the dynamism of his stage performances. In 1960 he came over from the States with Gene Vincent to tour

the country. His sound and stage persona took the country by storm; as did Vincent's, about which I wrote in a previous Russia'n'Roll column. I need to cover more of that 1960 tour later, for tragic reasons.

The first time I ever saw a film clip of Cochran was in the movie "The Girl Can't Help It." One could say a lot about that film. For example I could write a whole column about the effect of seeing Jayne Mansfield had on me and I'm sure I'm not the only guy! It was a brilliant rock'n'roll film and in it there is a magical clip of Eddie Cochran singing one of his own compositions, "Twenty flight rock." It's an unforgettable clip of a rockin' genius in action.

Although he was before my time in terms of when he was performing, as a young rock'n'roller he was the perfect role model to relate to. His image was that of a smartly dressed young social rebel. This was a persona many young working class boys like myself aspired to. And he certainly lived that life-style.

Although not quite as wild as his close friend Gene Vincent he nonetheless lived it up, in the short time he was a star up to his premature death. And unlike many other rockin' icons, the consensus amongst those who knew him personally is that he was a real nice guy. Glen Glenn, who was a friend of his, described him as follows: "Eddie was a fun guy to be around. We liked the same things. He liked to drink beer and chase women – although the women chased him when he had all his hit records. He had a lot of friends. Elvis was just the opposite, he was a lonely guy."

Now back to that 1960 UK tour. The previous year, 2 good friends of Eddie's and legends of rock'n'roll, Buddy Holly and Richie Valens, had been killed in a plane crash while on tour. The Big Bopper had also died in that tragedy. This affected Eddie greatly and family and friends say he developed a psychological premonition that he too would die young. He released a very famous song to commemorate his friends' deaths, "Three Stars". He decided he wanted to give up life on the road touring and instead spend his time recording music in the studio, thus reducing the chances of suffering a similar fate to his 2 friends. But he had to continue touring and performing, because basically he needed the money. So he agreed to tour Britain in 1960, along with his friend Gene Vincent.

The tour was a great success with the British audiences and one of the most memorable in rock'n'roll history. It certainly resurrected Gene Vincent's career as a super star, albeit relatively briefly due to Gene's ongoing problems with his critically injured leg and his alcoholism. But it wasn't a good experience for Eddie and Gene on a personal level. Jim Sullivan, who was part of the project, recalls the problems: "Eddie and Gene both seemed like very lost human beings. I don't think that Eddie wanted to be here for one minute. They both drank heavily. At one stage, Eddie was getting through a bottle of bourbon a day, if not two. At one point in the tour, he ended up with these great big blotches in his eyes caused by alcohol. Another time we had to prop him up at the Liverpool Empire where the microphone stand came up through a flap in the stage. We had to put his guitar over the microphone as it came up so he wouldn't fall over!"

It was towards the end of the tour that tragedy struck. Driving back in a taxi from a concert both he and Vincent had been performing in, the taxi was involved in a collision. The speeding car blew a tyre and crashed into a lamp post. Cochran, seated in the back, threw himself over his fiancée Sharon Sheeley to protect her. He was then thrown from the car when the door flew open. He died the following day of severe head injuries. Vincent survived the crash, but his already permanently damaged leg from an earlier accident became even worse as a result of his injuries. The taxi driver was convicted of dangerous driving but got off with a small fine.

In death Cochran became a sort of rock'n'roll martyr, especially to his fans in Britain. As a young rocker in the 1970s I can remember being caught

up in this feeling. There is a memorial stone commemorating his death in Rowden Hill, Chippenham (not far from Bath), where the accident happened. I went to visit it some years ago, during a period in my life when I didn't live all that far from the site. It was sort of a mark of respect to a rockin' legend. The stone is still there; it's not extravagant, but it's a real nice touch.

Eddie Cochran was sure special. He wrote and sang some of the greatest r'n'r songs of all time and the film clips of the time testify he was a great performer on stage, possessing charisma and raw energy. In the short time he was with us, he made his mark as one of the all-time rock'n'roll greats. He was "Somethin' Else!"

# THE HOTTEST ROCKIN'

# CHICK OF THEM ALL!

This month I'm going pay tribute to a rockin' 1950s icon, who in opinion was the greatest female rocker of them all. Many would disagree with my choice. For example I haven't chosen Wanda Jackson or Brenda Lee. In fact I suspect the name is one which will be new to a certain percentage of you.

On 18th April we organised a concert in Moscow at the prestigious Esse Cafe, in memory of this great singer (I hasten to add she is still with us, albeit in retirement for many a long year). She was Jo Ann Campbell and in the late 1950s sang and performed some of the greatest songs by any female rocker. "You're driving me mad", "Wassa matter with you" "Wait a minute", "Boogie woogie country girl" and "Motorcycle Michael" in my opinion are some of the greatest numbers ever recorded by any female singer in the history of rock'n'roll. Plus she really knew how to perform on stage.

As we were celebrating a female singer, my choice of performers just had to be the female icons of Russian rock'n'roll, the Marshmallows. Regular readers of my column in this magazine will know quite a bit about them. They're 3 beautiful and charismatic young women who sing and perform 1950s style r'n'r, with the support of 3 backing musicians. As they have done already quite a few times at the Esse Café, once more they wowed us with a great concert. Some of the photos you can see were taken at the event.

Like I said, Jo Ann Campbell was a great performer. Here is how Billy Poore, a writer and music promoter who lived through those times in the 1950s, describes his impressions the first time he saw her in action: "It wasn't just that outfit and them great looks. It was also what she was doin'. The way she rocked, shook, bumped and moved while playin' and slingin' her guitar around, as well as turnin' sideways and pointin' it atcha with a pout on her face while she was growlin' out this rockabilly tune I'd never heard, was just a killer memory that's lasted a whole lifetime for me. That was my first introduction to the wildest live stage female performer ever to belt out a rockabilly tune."

The rock'n'roll story of Jo Ann Campbell really begins in her early teens, when rock-'n'roll was in its infancy. Living in Jacksonville, Florida, she would tune in to one of the very few radio stations that were playing rock'n'roll at that time. Like many of her peers during that early period, the listening had to be done secretly when her parents were not around, as the music had a real bad reputation amongst that generation's parents. This is just another example of how revolutionary rock'n'roll was back then. It was the first really recognisable youth culture, which shocked and worried their parents.

Having got hooked on rock'n'roll, Jo Ann then began her career as a professional dancer. She had been learning dancing throughout her childhood and it was always the intention of her and her family that she should take it up professionally. She went to Europe on a big tour of the

United States Army bases, performing as a dancer for the American troops stationed there. On her return, she joined a dancing group, "the Johnny Conrad Dancers", and appeared regularly on US TV shows. She was still officially in High School at this time (she was 17) and the number of dance bookings she was getting made her leave school in 1955 to concentrate on her dancing career.

But in November 1955 an event occurred which changed her life. She happened to attend an Alan Freed rock'n'roll show at the New York Paramount Theatre. In previous articles I've written in this column covering the history of rock'n'roll, inevitably the name Alan Freed has kept popping up. He was a crucial figure in the early days of rock'n'roll, as a promoter and disc jockey. And sure enough he was about to play a crucial role in the career of Jo Ann Campbell. Here's how she described what happened at the show: "As that show went on and Alan Freed kept bringin' on acts like Frankie Lymon and the Teenagers, The Moonglows, The Cadillacs, Bill Haley and His Comets, Chuck Berry and

all the rest, it made me jump up and down and scream till I was dizzy. I mean kids were all out in the aisles and in front of the stage dancin' and just goin' crazy. Well, when I first came out of that first Alan Freed rock'n'roll show, I knew my days as a dancer were over, even though at the time I was up for parts in Broadway plays then. I was just determined I was gonna sing rock'n'roll and be on Alan Freed's stage one day. The next morning, I went into my manager's office and told him I wasn't gonna dance anymore and that I wanted to make a rock'n'roll record."

Fortunately for Jo Ann, her manager, although astonished

at her decision, had a few contacts in the music business and used them to try and get her started on a rock'n'roll career. She started performing, cut some records and her fame started to grow. Sure enough, Alan Freed got to hear about her, saw her in action and from then on signed her to all his rock'n'roll shows. This really was Jo Ann's golden period, when she was singing and performing at her rock'n'roll best.

Then in 1960 she made a decision which in hindsight even she regretted. She was signed to the ABC Paramount record label, one of the biggest recording companies in the World. She figured it was a big step towards super-stardom and for sure it did bring her some chart success for her records. But Paramount were not interested in real rock'n'roll and had her performing and recording much blander pop songs. She had been known as "Alan Freed's wild, rockin' gal" as a result of her tremendous performances on his shows, but now her style was much less rockin' and much more poppy. She continued performing until 1967, at which time she quit the business to concentrate on her family life.

Why not check out some of those earlier recordings by her. She was a female who could rock with the best, at a time when only a tiny percentage of rock'n'roll artists were women. For sure, there were other brilliant women rockers, like Wanda Jackson and Brenda Lee. But Wanda carried on way too long after her best days were over and Brenda wasn't rockin' enough for me. Don't get me wrong, both were very special, but I preferred Jo Ann. So here's to a unique female rocker - Jo Ann Campbell. As the title of one of her best albums named her, she was indeed "That Real Gone Gal"!

# THE TRUE KING OF ROCKABILLY

Who is the Rockabilly all-time King ? Some claim the title for Elvis Presley, based on his early years. Carl Perkins actually gave himself that title back in the 1960s. But as far as I'm concerned, the King was the one who stayed truer

to the authentic style and who cut the greatest rockabilly records of all time. And many, many rockabilly hep cats share my view.

His name was Charlie Feathers and on 16th May I organised a tribute concert here in Moscow at the prestigious Esse Jazz Cafe, to commemorate the rockabilly legend. I arranged for the Raw Cats to perform for us. I began the event with my rock'n'roll dance class. The Raw Cats

gave us a tremendous performance. I've written about them in an earlier column of "Russia'n'Roll", in particular their leader and vocalist / keyboard player, the Russian rockin' icon Valery Setkin: They really are a brilliant rock'n'roll band. Some of the photos you can see were taken at the concert.

Feathers was a real "Southern Boy". He was born in Mississippi in 1932 and as a rockabilly artist his greatest periods were during the times he recorded for the Sun and then the King Record labels. Those of you who really know your rock'n'roll history will recall the legendary status and contribution to rock'n'roll of the man who ran the Sun record label, Sam Phillips. Phillips played a key role in the early careers of the likes of Elvis Presley, Jerry Lee Lewis and Carl Perkins, to name but a few. But although he signed up Feathers to his record label, he didn't rate him much. He was happy to see him move to another label. Phillips claimed afterwards that Feathers should have stuck to pure Country music and would have been a big star. But Phillips misjudgement in this case has gotta rank as one of the few glaring errors in his otherwise uncanny and unique ability to find and nurture rock'n'roll genius!

Amazingly, when he began his musical career Feathers was almost illiterate and could hardly read or write. But his performances on stage and above all the quality of his music, were sensational. His style, especially his singing voice, can best be described as theatrical, hiccup-styled, energetic and charismatic. Have a listen for example on youtube to numbers like "Bottle to the Baby", "One Hand Loose" and "Everybody's Loving My Baby" and you'll see what I mean. These 3 songs of Feathers, along with others, rank as some of the greatest in rock'n'roll history. They're awesome.

He won acclaim amongst devotees of rockabilly, both during his greatest period of performing in the 1950s and then subsequently. But here's the thing.

Unlike Elvis and others like Carl Perkins, Charlie stayed true to the pure, unadulterated rockabilly style. So while these others earned greater fortune and fame by going more "mainstream", his sticking to his "roots" meant he didn't get the popularity and success he always felt he deserved. And indeed he did deserve it.

In fact to say that he believed he should have had more recognition is putting it mildly. He deeply resented the fact that stars like Presley and Perkins were getting the acclaim he felt he had earned. He knew Elvis well during their days together at Sun Records. As far as Charlie was concerned, Elvis' only great days musically were his early ones singing and performing rockabilly style numbers while at Sun Records.

It is also an understatement to say that Charlie was a difficult man to get along with. The stories are legion of him arguing and making enemies with music writers, booking agents, promoters, producers, music and record company executives, you name it! In addition, he was no saint: He had a string of convictions for illegal gambling activities.

Feathers was born into a poor Southern family. As a result his education suffered, hence the reason for his illiteracy. As a very young man, he had to work long hours at hard labour jobs, such as picking cotton or laying oil pipes.

He was typical of many of the truly great rock'n'rollers of the 1950s, such as Elvis, Carl Perkins and Jerry Lee Lewis, in that they too came from poor backgrounds. There really is a class element to this: Contrast their upbringings with those of the 1960s pop superstars. The likes of the Beatles and the Rolling Stones came from middle class families. Despite the "anti-establishment" image they tried to portray, these 60s groups were basically a bunch of middle class trendy lefties. Of course not every 50s rock'n'roll megastar had poor origins and not every 60s pop icon came from a well-to-do background, but certainly the majority did; which basically means there was generally something more honest and less hypocritical about the 50s rockers than those that came later.

And here's where it gets personal for me. In 1977 I saw the Great Man live in concert in London! It was an unforgettable event for me and also a revelation. The concert was at the Rainbow Theatre in London and the main reason I decided to go was to see Crazy Cavan, who were also on the bill. I remember being disappointed that the only ticket I could get was for a cheap seat right at the back in the upper tier, not only because of the inferior location but also because I'd been hoping maybe I could've got to do some jive dancing during the event in the lower tier! But my lasting impression from that concert, which included other rockin' icons such as Jack Scott, was Feathers. He was fantastic and still had that rockabilly magic touch. He also had a bit to say for himself in between songs and his comments were immensely interesting; predictably they were also laced with resentment that he hadn't been given more acknowledgement during his career and he again expressed disappointment at the way Elvis' career developed after his Sun Records days.

Charlie has become a hero to devotees of rockabilly music, not only because of the brilliance of his music but also because unlike so many others he stayed true to the original authentic rockabilly sound. By the late 1980s his health had rapidly deteriorated. He developed a very severe form of diabetes and for the last decade of his life, although he continued to perform and make records, didn't fully recover. He died in 1998 of a stroke-induced coma. And despite his difficult personality which made him constantly complain about his being "under-valued" as a rockin' icon, he was indeed right in thinking he deserved even more acclaim and legendary status than he got. Here's to you, Charlie; the King of Rockabilly!

# THE LIFE AND TIMES OF A RUSSIAN ROCK'N'ROLL LEGEND

This month let me introduce you to another Russian rock'n'roll legend. His story is an important one, not just because of his status in Russia but because his story is an excellent example of someone living the rock'n'roll life to the full.

Alexey "Lex" Blokhin is a larger than life rockin' icon who is loud, brash, with a chequered past and is not ashamed of it. His colourful life includes a term of imprisonment in a United States prison. He has, as the saying goes, ruffled a few feathers along the way and has acquired many friends and a few enemies; his story below will show examples of this. He has certainly mellowed since his wild and crazy days in the 1990s, but one of the great things about Lex is – he still brings an element of the "wild and crazy" into his performances on stage. Regular readers of this column will know that I like my music on the wilder side and Alexey certainly comes into this category. He's a great character who has contributed so much to Russian rock'n'roll. His status as a performer is unquestioned; he's been a rock'n'roll star in Russia over a long period of time. His story tells us not only about him, but about the history of Russian

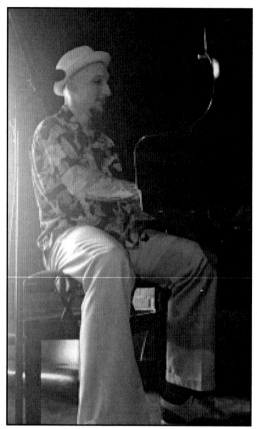

rock'n'roll music over the last generation, as well as being a fascinating insight into Russia generally during this period of time.

On 13th June I booked him to perform for us at the premier Moscow venue of the Esse Café in Moscow. As usual he gave a larger than life, rockin' performance. He is a rock'n'roll star and is not backwards in letting everyone know it. His performance at the Café was terrific. Some of the photos you can see were taken at the Café. His speciality is vocals and keyboards.

I spent some time with Lex, discussing his rock'n'roll life and below are the results. He didn't tell me much about his life in prison whilst serving a sentence in the USA, except to say that the experience improved his English language skills! I'll let him tell you his story.

"Thank you for your interest in my rock'n'roll story, Richard! My musical story begins when I was a young boy in the old Soviet Union (I was born in 1973). My parents had good musical tastes. Back then in the USSR "Western" music was frowned upon so LP's were rare. But my family had tapes of jazz and pop music of that time. In my early childhood I heard Abba, Tom Jones, Frank Sinatra, Cliff Richard and many others. My Mom, who's 82 now, still prefers Cliff Richard over Elvis.

I started studying piano from the age of 4 years old. In 1980 I entered a children's music school and began singing in the children's choir. The music classes took place in the evenings, in the same school building where I was studying in the daytime. At the school I attended as a boy, they had pianos in every classroom (this was not all that unusual in Russia at that time). Every break between classes I played those pianos. So my schoolmates became my first audience. I got lots of practise and besides the girls were really diggin' me! I also started composing my own songs in the Russian language.

I discovered real rock-n-roll at the age of 13. Or was it 14? I don't remember the exact wheres or whens, but it must have been a good day 'cause I haven't been tired of this music yet!

At the age 15 I visited the USA for the first time in my life. For a boy who'd grown up in USSR that was quite a shock. Big cars, big buildings, bright lights and friendly people, as opposed to the way that the Soviet mass media portrayed them. And music! All kinds of it: traditional and modern, rock, jazz, country, blues – loads and loads of delicious food for the soul. When I came

 back I brought with me dozens of tapes.

At 15 I joined my first rock'n'roll band. They needed an accordion player to be able to re-create the sound without using electricity. I promised that I would buy an accordion later and meanwhile we started rehearsals with me on piano. Eventually I stayed on piano. The band was called "Gavayskie Ostrova" (Hawaii Islands). We were wearing bright-colored shirts, mostly handmade by our Mums. Back in those days one couldn't get a decent Hawaian shirt in the Soviet Union. The band played mainstream rock-n-roll, with some twist music thrown in.

By that time many things in the USSR started to change. The Cold War was rolling to an end. So loudly dressed school kids who played "capitalist" music attracted the attention of Soviet TV and radio. I shouldn't say that we became popular, but we sure got known. Despite this, "Hawaian Islands" never made a decent record.

I have to point out that we didn't play music for a living. All of us lived with our parents and prepared to go to colleges. In Russia military service is compulsory for all males who turn 18 and lasts for two years. One of the ways to avoid getting into the army was to go to college. That's how the Government encouraged more people to get higher education. Such stimulation is now lost in modern day Russia, but that's a whole other story.

So "Hawaian Islands" went on hiatus, as we were getting ready for our colleges. The band never got together again, and of all it's members only I continued playing music. God knows whether that was a wise decision or not.

It was the last year of Soviet Union. Of course we didn't know that, but there was that spirit in the air. Everybody just became sharper, edgier, more emotional, more aggressive. I also was an "angry young man" by that time. And I wanted a new band which would play faster, more energetic music. And that band was formed in April. We called it "Crazy Man Crazy" after Bill Haley's song. Later the spelling was changed to "Krazy Men Krazy". Of course that sounded incorrect, but who cares? We were all rebels, weren't we? The band started playing traditional rockabilly with a lot of "pumping" piano. Later on we inclined towards a more neo-rockabilly sound and even used some elements of psychobilly. We composed our own songs. That's when I started writing songs in English.

"Krazymen" started making money big time, as I thought in those days. Contrary to Hollywood movies we don't have snowy winters all year round.

In the Spring of 1991 we started playing on Moscow streets. That's how the band got cash and a following amongst Moscow youngsters. Electricity was not used so I just sang. Sometimes I played rhythm guitar, occasionally bass or drums when anybody in the rhythm-section was absent at the time. Besides this, "Krazymen" played regular "electric" gigs with me on the piano. We played whenever and wherever we could, for any audience who would care to listen. Pretty soon it paid off. We were chosen as a backing band for the English rock'n'roll singer and piano player Dave Taylor during his visit to the USSR. Later on we went to Finland. The very first abroad tour in my life was not a big success, but hey, that was not too bad for a band that was less than a year old.

By the end of the summer, the Soviet Union collapsed and things started getting more crazy day by day. Suddenly everybody was obsessed with making money. I was no exception. I got an evening job, at one of the Moscow restaurants where I played requests. I worked in turns with Denis Mazhukov, who is now the Russian King of Rock'n'Roll, as he calls himself.

At the college I was among the worst scholars but it didn't bother me much. I played music every night either on the job or with my band. Krazy Men Krazy became quite popular and gathered a considerable following. Crowds gathered at the shows, even though back then there was no such thing as the Internet.

From 1992 to 1995 "Krazy Men Krazy" recorded five albums, three of them exclusively in English. All of them were issued on tape and still are in circulations among fans. In 1994 the compilation of English-language material was issued on CD and to this day this is the only record left.

In 1995 I finally graduated. Needless to say, I never thought about an accounting career and wanted to keep on playing music. By that time I got tired of my band's neo-rockabilly sound. It was the year when I heard the record of Louis Prima. I tried to change the band's course towards jumpin' jive, but my bandmates were not very enthusiastic about it. So at the end of the year I quit the band and started forming my own jumpin' jive and neo-swing outfit. After several name changes the project was called "Ruby Stars". The band existed for a year and a half. It was very hard to keep the line-up steady. The general economic situation in Russia was worsening and it influenced showbiz. Sometimes there were ten people on stage and other times I had to play the bass line on the synth with my left hand and beside me there was only a drummer and a sax player. "Ruby Stars" started recording an album but never completed it.

In 1997 I got a proposal to go to the USA as an interpreter for a group of businessmen. I planned to make some money for my music recording process from the trip and also to see the country. After my two week duties were done, I spontaneously decided not to come back.

In the States I spent almost five years. Those were crazy but eventful years. I was in jail for cheque fraud. I played bass in an Uzbekistan restaurant, I learned Spanish and Italian. I built houses, washed cars, made jewelry, moved and assembled furniture. I did a lot of things. The only thing I didn't do in the USA – I didn't play rock'n'roll. Although eventually I ended up playing keyboards and sometimes bass for electronic, ethnic, hard rock and even punk bands, but none of them was a real rock'n'roll band.

By the beginning of the century 21, I was quite tired of being an immigrant. I didn't have a steady job nor my own home. And my friends in Moscow wrote to me how good the life was over there. For some time I was uncertain, should I return to Russia ? But then it happened, the destruction of the World Trade Center in September 11, 2001. As I watched the fire from my roof in New York City, I made my decision. On November 4, 2001 my voyage came to an end.

Upon my return I formed a new band by the old name "Ruby Stars". We played mostly rock'n'roll hits along with some songs of our own. All in all the second incarnation of Ruby Stars wasn't very successful, although we once played at a private party for the Russian government (yes, I saw Pres. Putin quite close-up). I sensed that the band lacked some kinda "punch" about it, something that people could remember.

In 2003 my old friends and colleagues decided to form a neo-swing band and invited me to be a front man. I gladly agreed. This band got the name "Lexicon Orchestra". Initially the spelling was supposed to be "Lex' Icon Orchestra" but my bandmates dropped the idea. I sang and played keys with "Lexicon Orchestra" for three years. Those years left mixed impressions for me. On the positive side, the band played good music, the kind that I liked. We were playing gigs, going on tours over Russia and abroad, a lot of private parties. The management was good, and we got paid well. We played some songs in Spanish and Italian and for Russia it was a new style.

At the same time there was a certain tension between me and some band members. They thought that I was acting like a star and showed off. But isn't a front man supposed to show off? A candid, bland singer won't attract any audience. There also was an issue of creativity. I wrote some songs especially for the band, and at first we played them at our gigs. But later all my songs were dumped in favor of more and more covers and jazz-standards. And to make things worse, very frequent gigs and rehearsals caused problems with my vocal chords.

Things got worse and worse until in the beginning of 2006 I quit the band and got a day job that had nothing to do with music. I started working on TV, translating English and Spanish-language films and series into Russian. But I didn't plan to give up my music career. My day job gave me the necessary time to start a new band. I called it "Lex & Team", sometimes it's referred to as "Lex E Komanda" in Russian.

What can I say? Finally my dreams came true. I write songs and play them, still I haven't forgotten good ol' rock'n'roll hits. In my songs I used elements of different styles from salsa to folk songs but the base of them all is traditional swinging rhythm.

My band plays quite often all over Russia and abroad, but not too often so we don't get weary. Besides I play a lot as a session–man with many Russian musicians or with foreign performers when they come to Russia. Right now I'm working on an album where my best songs for the last 25 years will be presented in a new sound.

My favorite rock'n'rollers: Gene Vincent (only early records), Johnny Burnette, Freddy "Fingers" Lee, Buddy Holly, Eddie Cochran, Jerry Lee Lewis (only early records), Elvis (not seventies), Bill Haley (only early records), Brian Setzer, Mark Harman, Steve Whitehouse

Favorite swingers: Louis Prima, Cab Calloway, Louis Jordan, Dean Martin

Favorite rockers: Slade, Asia, Deep Purple, ELP, Beatles & Sir Paul McCartney, Mick Green.

Rock'n'Roll is still the way of life for me. If someday you're in the vicinity and have nothing to do, come see my show on a Saturday night. I promise you won't ever regret it!

Thank you for your story, Alexey! Catch some of the Lex Magic yourself, at www.lexmusic.su

# THE ORIGINAL REBEL

On 18th July here in Moscow we organised a Tribute Concert to a real Legend. It was to an American icon who was not even a rock'n'roll performer, but whose legacy and image were perhaps more important to 1950s rock'n'roll youth culture than anyone else.

His name was James Dean. He appeared in a few Hollywood films in the early 1950s, but he hit mega-stardom with his performances in his last 3 movies, "East of Eden", "Rebel without a Cause" and "Giant". It was above all Rebel without a Cause, released in 1955, which really established him as the quintessential teenage rebel.

We booked the famous Russian rock'n'roll band the Great Pretenders to perform for us on 18th July at the Esse Café in Moscow. Readers of this column will know how big they are in Russian rock'n'roll. We had a great concert

and a fitting tribute to the original Rebel. Some of the photos you can see were taken at the Event.

Those of us who grew up with rock'n'roll can testify to the personal impact of Dean and not just on those who were teenagers in the 1950s. My teenage years came later, but I can still remember the Dean image that we all tried, in our different ways, to cultivate. John Lennon once famously said, "without Jimmy Dean the Beatles would never have existed". Martin Sheen described his legacy for young people, "Marlon Brando changed the way actors acted. James Dean changed the way people lived".

Above all it was Dean's persona as the ultimate rebel, for example in terms of the generation gap between parents and teenagers, that transformed him into a legend. This theme was in evidence in the movie East of Eden but it was Rebel without a Cause that was the defining moment of his acting career. In viewing the film, one always needs to judge it according to the time it was made. By today's standards, the dialogue and story line might seem tame, but not in 1955. It was revolutionary, in that it covered themes hitherto not dealt with in films. It's coverage of the generational conflict between teenagers and parents was ground breaking for its time and it turned Dean into a hero and role model for young people in America and the Western World generally. It dealt with the need to prove oneself to one's peers (in this case a teenage gang)

and Dean's character in the movie went through a "test" to prove he was no coward. The romantic angle is covered of course, with the famous Natalie Wood playing the female role opposite Dean.

I won't go into any more detail about the plot of the movie itself, since many of you have seen it already. Those that haven't can view it on youtube. Dean's charisma and personality shine throughout the film, in a way that make it hard to think of any other actor with such a powerful on-screen presence. From the time of its release, teenagers started to identify with Dean. Add to this the explosive mix of rock'n'roll music, which came onto the scene at about the same time and you can imagine the tremendous effect it had on American and Western society.

The genesis of the idea for the film came from the director Nicholas Ray. He wanted to make a movie about the teenage social rebellion taking place at that time and to show it was not just a small minority of under-privileged youth involved. His movie demonstrated that this rebellious permeated all classes of society, including within middle class families. Ray recognised that an authentic film on this subject would need to have lots of input from teenagers themselves. He therefore gave a lot free rein to the teenage actors in the movie, to come up with ideas, concepts, etc., that could be used in the picture. Above all he used Dean in this way, someone who really was an authentic youth rebel. Dean, although only 24 years old at the time, was encouraged by Ray to take on the role of an unofficial co-director of the movie and this factor was one of the key elements that made it such an exponential success.

Plus there were lots of spicy details happening off-screen as well as on. Natalie Wood, then only 16, was having an affair with the 44 year old Ray. Wood and Dean were both definitely attracted to each other, but Wood's affair with the director prevented it going too far. Dean's most important romantic relationship had occurred earlier, in the early 1950s, when he dated the Italian actress Pier Angeli. She was the love of his life and Dean wanted to marry her. But the movie studio MGM brought heavy pressure to bear on him not to do so, on the grounds that it would have a negative effect on his film star image. After he advised Pier of this, Dean then went to New York for some acting work and it was there he read in the newspapers that she had announced she was going to marry the famous singer Vic Damone. The whole affair had a big negative impact on Dean. And Angeli's story is not a happy one: She had another failed marriage after the one with Damone ended and she committed suicide, by taking a drug overdose in 1971 at the age of 39. Three years before she died, she made public that the main reason for her unhappiness was the ending of her relationship with Dean: "He is the only man I ever loved deeply as a woman should love a man. I never loved either of my husbands the way I loved Jimmy."

Dean lived a socially wild life off-screen. His behaviour was erratic, he loved fast cars and generally lived life on the edge. This of course only endeared him even more to his young fans. The actor Paul Lucas who worked with him, at the time said "this son of a bitch is absolutely crazy". Another who knew him in the 1950s, Dennis Stock, described him thus, "he lived like a stray animal. Come to think of it he was a stray animal."

One of his favourite quotes was "to me the only success, the only greatness, is immortality". And, already a legend, his final act secured his immortality in the memory of future generations of fans. He was a huge car racing enthusiast and had a reputation for driving "on the edge". He accepted the risks of driving in this way and when discussing the possibility of a fatal crash, responded with "what better way to die ? It's fast and clean and you go out in a blaze of glory." He also had a premonition that he would die before he was 30. His credo was "live fast, die young."

In September 1955, driving to a car racing event in California, Dean was again speeding and ignored a red light. He crashed into another vehicle and was killed almost instantly. He was only 24 years old. The manner of his death only added to his iconic status amongst his young fans. He achieved a kind of "martyrdom" in death: He lived and died in the life style that so many of the youth at that time and in later generations aspired to.

Many films and records were made about him over the years after his death and his legend still lives on. As time passed, some stories stated about his personal life were the opposite of his sexual image, but regardless of whether some of them were true or not, it is unquestioned that his legacy to the rock'n'roll generation was huge. As Andy Warhol famously described him, "it might be innocence struggling with experience, youth with age, or man with his image. But in every aspect his struggle was a mirror to a generation of rebels without a cause."

# RUSSIA'S WILDEST CAT

Here in Russia, we have many top quality rock'n'roll bands. This month I'm gonna focus on the leader of the one of the very best. He can truly be described as one of the most charismatic, larger than life and in rock'n'roll terms a real Wild Cat.

His group is the Raw Cats, about whom I've written before in this column. The Wild Cat in question is Valery Setkin, a man with a long and famous history on the rockin' scene. I have booked him myself to perform at the Esse Café in Moscow on many occasions. Every time he went down a storm. In Russian rock'n'roll he is a real legend. The stories about him are also legion. They tend to be raunchy and rather more than (to use a cinema term) "PG"-rated. You will hear some of them below, with some of the more adult-oriented stories included, albeit the really hard-core ones have had to be deleted! I sat down with Valery to hear his fascinating rockin' story. Here it is, in his own words:

I felt the rock'n'roll spirit when I was a child. My father brought me the vinyl records of Elvis and Jerry Lee and I was dancing in my playpen, listening to them. About the Raw Cats, it was in the middle of 2004. I was drinking, because my girlfriend decided to leave me and my double bass player went to a rival band named the Beat Devils. But then I said "Sod the lot of 'em" - I'm rock'n'roll and as long as I live, I will be playing this music. I took my drummer from my early project named the Old Ladies Band. I put out an advert and found a double bass player; the funniest thing was that he was the Beat Devils' original bass player. And the guitarist was a friend of my drummer. So the Raw Cats were formed, to the glory of Rock'n'Roll!

I wasn't really influenced musically by other Russian rock'n'roll groups, my only influences were Elvis, Jerry Lee, Johnny Burnette, Gene Vincent, Eddie Cochran, Johnny Cash and of course Brian Setzer!

There have been many significant events in the history of the Raw Cats. I think the biggest ones have been our birthday party events. I thank all our fans that are listening and coming to our concerts.

But I remember some special shows. The first one was when we were performing as a support act at a Red Elvises' Concert in 2006 (I don't remember which month) at the Orange Club in Moscow [at this point I need to explain – the Red Elvises were a hugely popular band in Russia at that time. Continue, Valery]. And we outdid them. That was a brilliant concert, I was singin' like the real Elvis, my band was playing awesomely and the crowd was crazy and furious. And the next day I saw the reviews on social media; all the people who'd been present at the concert said that the "first band was much better than the megastar Red Elvises."

One more great show was in 2009 (I think that was the year). It was the day of Elvis Presley's birthday. And we were performing at the prestigious B1 Club in Moscow, to celebrate the legend's birthday. The headliner of the event was Jack Baymoore and his Bandits (the Swedish rockabilly icons of "AV8 Boogie" fame). When he heard our band playing, he went to the sound engineer, kicked

him out of his place and started to run our sound system, because he wanted all the people to hear the correct sound of our music!

Richard, you asked me for some interesting or amusing stories connected with the band. Some I've already given you [regular readers of this column will remember my previous article some time ago about the Raw Cats and the wild, crazy stories linked to Valery. One in particular concerned a beautiful young Russian woman by the name of Polina, performing an unforgettable striptease at a Raw Cats' gig. Continue, Valery] Well this next story is connected with one I've already provided you. It was a couple of years ago. We were performing at the Rhythm'n'Blues Café. So, your favourite Raw Cats' fan Polina (who was the "official stripper" the Raw Cats) and her friend Katya went under the stage and turned their backs to the crowd. They then took off their blue jeans and showed everybody the logo of the Raw Cats, tattooed on their bare bums; both of them had one on their left bum cheek and one on their right!

And Richard, you asked me for some tasty stories outside of the Raw Cats, during my time in Russian rock'n'Roll. I think I can tell one [Valery has very many of them; unfortunately as advised above most of them are unrepeatable in a magazine!]. My friend Benny Blues called me to play with his band in 2010 in Sevastopol (in Crimea) at the Bike show, that was organised by the Night Wolves Bike Club of Russia. So, we played there and next morning I asked him to go with me to a students' camp near Alushta, that I was visiting every year, from 2005 to 2010. It's a helluva place, with port wine, lots of beautiful female students, near the sea, you get the picture! So we traveled there for the day. I really wanted to get there and so we arrived. I met there several of my friends, at the famous bar named "The Mole". And we were drinkin' and dancin'. Benny fell asleep and I met the dawn in with champagne with everybody, but not Benny. And then I decided to walk up to the mountain, where I usually set my tent. I went there and fell sleep in the bushes. Benny woke up and didn't find me. He tried without success to find me, then went away by taxi to Sevastopol. I woke up, finding myself with an awful hangover, without any money, without my passport, without a shirt, only in shorts and 300 kilometers away from Sevastopol. I had about 8 hours to get to our flat and to go to our train to Moscow. And I did it. I traveled to Alushta, there found a man, who decided to drive me to Sevastopol. I didn't even know the address of the street where Benny was. I navigated on my memory. But I damn well did it. And we got on that train to Moscow five minutes before it was due to leave.

What were the main reasons for the Raw Cats' big success over the last 11 years ? I think it's only because of my singing and performing from the deepest depths of my soul, that is fuelled with love, women I've loved and of course Whisky. And hard, hard, hard work.

Changes to the personnel of the group during the history of the band ? Well, to play in the Raw Cats band is really hard work, so some guys said that was enough rock'n'roll for them and left. And some left for health reasons. About significant personal differences amongst the group's members over the years, well I can advise the following. I had several problems in my group with double bass players. But I don't want to speak about it. I'm grateful to all who were playing with me during these 11 years.

As to my own personal musical history, outside of the Raw Cats, I started playing piano when I was a kid. I graduated from one school, then went to a Jazz college in Russia, where I grew up as a real musician. Best wishes to my teacher Odyssey Bogusevich, who taught me not to think about what I'm playing the next second! In 1999 I was at the concert of the Red Hot Chilli Peppers. I had a lot of vodka that evening, had a fight with a skinhead and with a bruise under my right eye I met a beautiful girl named Sveta. We had a romance and she arranged for me to join the band of her friends, who were playing something like Oasis. So after several rehearsals I performed in my first concert. It was at the Wild West Club and it's true to say the Club had never seen such a show. I was sort of a "great balls of fire" on the stage and was NOT playing in the Oasis style. After two months predictably I was kicked out the band, because I was too rock'n'roll for them. Then I met a friend of mine, who was the leader of the blues band Moby Dick. I had studied in jazz college with the band's bass player, Volodya. I did a few jam sessions with them and kept in contact. After a while the group Moby Dick collapsed and they said to me "OK, you're a cool guy, let's work together". With them I formed the "Old Ladies Band" and after that the Raw Cats. Life's a funny thing.

Richard, you asked me to name any individuals in the history of Russian rock'n'roll that I particularly admire, for their contribution to the rockin' scene here in Russia. Well, here's one. I admire Muslim Magomaev. He was an honorable member of the Elvis Presley fan club in Russia. He was the Russian Elvis I think. He was a great Russian singer and he had a great voice, he was also an awesome musician. I was listening to his songs in cartoon films when I was a kid. I grew up on his music.

My all-time rock'n'roll heroes are Elvis, Jerry Lee, Johnny Cash and the Stray Cats. Why ? Because they brought me to rock'n'roll, which is the style of my life and everything that I love. My all-time favourite rock'n'roll song is I think Jailhouse Rock: if my choice had to be a ballad then "I can't help falling in Love".

I am optimistic about the future of Russian rock'n'roll. Of course I'm optimistic: "As long as I live, I wanna give you all of my heart, can't be apart. As long as I live, I wanna give you the stars above that shine. Give just me a little more time and I'll make this whole World yours and mine."

Thank you, Valery. A nice touch to end on some lyrics from a great song! To catch some of the Setkin magic, you can go to the Raw Cats' web-site at http://www.rawcats.ru/ As long as Valery is around, Russian rock'n'roll will never die!

November 2015

# RED AND ROCKIN'

This month I can report on an exciting new development in Russian Rock'n'Roll. The scene has become enhanced with the arrival of relatively new kids on the block. Although the personnel of the group in question have been on the music scene for a while, it is only fairly recently they've set up a great new rock'n'roll band. The band is Red Rox and on 12th September I booked them to perform at the Esse Café in Moscow.

The concert was a blast. Many of those present who hadn't seen them perform before were blown away by their high energy performance. It was their first gig at the Esse Café and it sure won't be the last. Some of the photos you can see were taken at the concert. Plus, you can see the concert on youtube: Go to youtube and type in the search engine "Red Rox - Jazz Club Esse".

The line-up of the band usually comprises 5 or 6 performers, including a saxophonist, drummer and trumpeter. But the regular unchanging members are Evgeny Sheyko (lead guitar), Roman Lukinykh (vocals) and Alex

Nikitin (upright bass). The group uses session musicians to cover the other instruments.

I sat down with Evgeny, the leader of the band, shortly after the concert and we talked Red Rox. Here is the group's story, told by Evgeny:

Well Richard, first of all to give your readers an idea of our style of music, here are some examples of the songs we perform the most: Elvis Presley - All shook up, Carl Perkins - Blue suede shoes, Johnny Cash - Folsom prison blues, Jerry Lee Lewis - Great balls of fire, Hank Williams - Hey, Good Lookin', Chuck Berry - Johnny B Goode, Bill Haley - Rock around the clock, Tennessee Ernie Ford - Sixteen tons. I think you get the picture! We also compose and perform our own rock'n'roll songs. Here are 3 of them, "Coming home", "Definitely wild" and "Dirty song". I would describe the musical style of Red Rox as rock'n'roll, rockabilly, rhythm'n'blues and swing.

How did we first get into rock'n'roll and what is the story of how Red Rox got together? Well, that's a long story. Together with Roman we formed our first group in 2005. He suggested we call it "Red Rox", but we finally decided on "Lucky Seven". We played country, rock'n'roll and hard rock. Unluckily, for various reasons the group ended up not performing at all and both of us got involved in different musical projects. We then met at a Blues Jam at the Roadhouse Bar in Moscow in December 2009 and decided to try again. Roma called me on the phone on Elvis's birthday (8th January) and recommended we form a rock'n'roll band. We got musicians from our past groups. I brought the bass player and Roman brought the piano man. Together we found a drummer and started to perform blues covers, some rock'n'roll covers and Russian rock covers. Roman insisted we call our group "Red Rox". He explained the meaning of "Rox" as some kind of "rockin' fox".

As to our musical influences, interestingly my first inspiration was Jimi Hendrix. Roman was influenced by classic country and Elvis Presley, the bass player and the drummer more by Russian rock groups. The piano player liked jazz and Ray Charles. However, Red Rox passed through plenty of time, so our influences also were changing. For example, when we started to play rockabilly, we enjoyed the Wise Guys, Hi Tones, Rawcats 88, etc, (Russian rock-'n'roll bands); now we are fond of JD McPherson, Hillbilly Moon Explosion, the Baseballs and High Noon.

Many things, significant and otherwise, have occurred in Red Rox's history. Here are 2 significant ones. The first event changed my musical world. Our first bass player (Slava), Roman and me went to a new rock'n'roll bar called "Grease" in Moscow, where we first saw people who looked like they were from the fifties. That's where I first saw you, Richard. [Evgeny is right. The Grease Club was a favourite hang out for rock'n'rollers like myself in Moscow. A truly great club. We sorely miss the fact it is no longer a rock'n'roll club. Continue, Evgeny]. The groups were playing like in the fifties and everybody was dancing jive. Me and Slava had long hair before that event. But after that, we decided to play only rockabilly and change our images. We cut our

hair, bought the grease for our hair and some fancy clothes. Slava bought an upright bass.

The second event was when I met Alex Nikitin, our current upright bass player. We were playing at a Marshmallows concert (the Marshmallows, another terrific Russian rock'n'roll group). I met him at the rehearsal. I've never seen a better upright player, and I swore to myself that he will play in my band. Gladly some years after, I achieved this goal. I founded a new hillbilly trio and invited him to join it. You know, today Red Rox still perform only because of "Twenty Fifty". [I need to explain here. Twenty Fifty is the name of the 3 piece hillbilly group. Evgeny, Roman and Alexey run and perform in both groups i.e. Red Rox and Twenty Fifty. Continue, Evgeny]. In most of the concerts, we perform as a trio. I can explain it only by the economic situation: A lot of the venues in Russia have substituted live music for such things as karaoke, a cheaper alternative. So today some of the places for us to perform are pubs and bars that cannot pay for such big groups as Red Rox. [Another explanation here from Richard: This economic situation is partly the result of the unfair and totally unnecessary sanctions imposed on Russian by Western countries including the UK. So these stupid Western sanctions on Russia are even hitting Rock'n'Roll!]

There are many interesting / amusing stories connected with the band. Here's one.

Once we went to play at a private party on the Selegare Lake (a long distance from Moscow). I rented a trailer / caravan and a driver to minimise the risks, because of the state of the Russian roads and the cold, snowy weather. We were asleep most of the time on the journey, although it was very cold inside the trailer. One of us asked the driver to turn on the heater. "No problem", said the driver and turned on the air conditioner. All of us started to shiver with cold, and shouted "turn the goddamn heater higher!". He then proceeded to turn the air conditioner up even higher and we froze even more. He eventually discovered his mistake. But the funniest thing (although not at the time) was, he continued to make the same mistake 5 /6 times more during the journey. I was sleeping when one of the trailer's wheels got stuck in a hole in the road and the vehicle jolted sharply. I woke up because of intense pain and a loud cracking noise, followed by laughter from my companions. My body was lying underneath most of the musical instruments which had fallen on top of me. However, it's not the end of the story. Our customer's villa was in the forest and the road was rather wet. Anyway, we made it there and performed a great concert, getting plenty of money. We finished late at night and began the journey home. It became very cold, so the road through the forest got totally frozen. Now in Russia all vehicle owners change their tyres into winter ones, with small bits of metal in them, to enable the vehicles to operate in the cold Russian winters. But our driver said "my Mum told me changing summer tyres to winter ones was a silly idea." In retrospect it must have been funny (although not at the time for us) to see five musicians pushing the trailer over a long distance through the deep forest just to get back home.

I believe the 2 main reasons for our success on the rock'n'roll scene are hard rehearsals and great musicians. In the band's history there's been quite a

few personnel changes. We changed 9 drummers, 4 bass players, 5 saxophonists, and a piano player left us to get a job in Munich. It was always a huge problem when somebody left the group, we had to learn all the songs again and refuse concerts till we got it sorted. So we've changed our policy. Today Red Rox comprises the 3 of us - myself, Roman and Alex - and the rest are session players. The group has also had its share of personal differences. For example, our first bass player Slava always refused to learn modern songs and always lost his mind if there were only a few people at our concerts, or if the concert was not really successful. Four times he physically kicked our drummers when we were performing. Eventually he left to join the Russian group Diamond Hand.

Here are our biggest musical influences: Roman – Elvis, Alex – Johnny Burnette, Me – Johnny Bach and the Moonshine Boozers. All-time rock'n'roll heroes ? Roman - Elvis (he is the King), Johnny Cash (texts and rhythm), Jerry Lee Lewis (burning piano): Me - Lemmy Kilmister from Motorhead. I bought their album "Overkill" once and it completely turned my mind. I used to listen to heavy metal mostly, but after Overkill I realised that I love rock'n'roll. I began to study this musical direction, began to discover new artists and finally I found rockabilly music. So if you ask - Why Lemmy? I'll answer that because of him, I am what I am today. And Alex – "Johnny Burnette 'cause he was far ahead of his time and today he is still relevant."

As to our all-time favourite songs, well mine is Johnny B Goode. In Russia we all love this song and everyone is happy to hear it again and again. So as trivial as it may sound, if we're playing rock'n'roll, we just have do Johnny B. Roman - Johnny B Goode, for sure! We finalise every concert with this song. Alex - Johnny Horton's "I'm coming home".

There are some individuals in the history of Russian rock'n'roll that I particularly admire, for their contribution to the rockin' scene here in Russia. A great upright bass player Timur Popovkin is kind of a legend, he played highly professionally in the best rockabilly bands in Russia. Alex "The Fat one" Nikitin knows personally every rockabilly bass player in the World [by the way, about that nickname – Alex is especially tall and especially skinny!]. And every one of them plays only on Alex's upright bass while staying and performing in Moscow. Vladimir Khoruzhiy from the Hi Tones is really a rock'n'roll legend, everybody here knows him. He is a super authentic guitar player! Roman likes Denis Majhukov for his real rockin' piano; Denis performed with Chuck Berry twice. However, we respect all the rock'n'roll, rockabilly, hillbilly groups, 'cause while they playing it – rock'n'roll lives.

I am optimistic about the future of Russian rock'n'roll. Why not! I've seen a few young groups over the last few months. They did pretty good. Rock-'n'Roll will always be, 'cause nothing is more danceable and energetic. Everybody in every little town somehow heard songs such as Rock around the Clock, Never can tell, or Tutti-Frutti. Today Rock'n'Roll is classic. We all know that Classics never die!

Thank you Evgeny, for a great story. And Thanks to Red Rox, for enriching our rockin' scene over here in the East!